SOUTH-WEST SCOTLAND

TOM ATKINSON

Who's for Tongland?

Visit Tongland Hydro-Electric Power Station for a fascinating insight into electrical power and how it is made.

Watch our audio-visual presentation, see the dramatic turbine hall and the salmon fish ladder.

We provide free transport from Kirkcudbright and back.

FREE GUIDED TOURS:
Mon to Sat 10 am, 11.30 am, 2 pm, 3.30 pm, anyday during the summer except Sundays.

TELEPHONE BOOKINGS ONLY
'Phone Kirkcudbright 30114 between 10 am and 12.30 pm, 2 pm and 4 pm.

·GALLOWAY· HYDRO SCHEME·

SSEB Electricity

Life would be dull without it.

SOUTH-WEST SCOTLAND

TOM ATKINSON

Published by
LUATH PRESS Ltd.
Barr, Ayrshire.

MALIN COURT

Maidens, Turnberry, Ayrshire.

Malin Court has been described as an oasis of comfort on the shores of the Atlantic, providing quiet luxury away from the hurly-burly of everyday living. Guests are assured of 'Good Food' pleasantly served in a rather special restaurant looking to the Island of Arran and the hills beyond.

Our Restaurant and Bar Lounge can be uniquely integrated to provide the ideal setting for weddings, private parties, annual dinners, smokers, 21st birthdays, silver weddings — even small conferences and seminars.

Our bedrooms are extremely comfortable and are complete with private facilities of bath, shower, bidet, toilet and wash-hand basin together with television, telephone and radio.

Dinner is served from 7.30 p.m. in the relaxing atmosphere of our main Restaurant with enchanting views across the Firth of Clyde to Ailsa Craig and the romantic Isle of Arran. Luncheons are served in the Restaurant from 1.00 p.m. To complement our excellent *a la carte* and *table d'hote* menus, we offer an extensive selection of choice wines. Our menus are changed daily, and all dishes are silver-served.

Attractive Bar Lunches are also available daily in our lounge.

For both Hotel and Restaurant Reservations, please telephone: Turnberry (065 53) 457.

This is the second book in the Series
'Guides to Western Scotland'

First Edition 1982
Second Impression, 1982
Revised Edition 1983
Revised Edition 1984
Revised Edition 1985
Revised Edition 1986

The border on the cover is a Celtic design,
based upon what was probably a Pictish original.

© Luath Press Ltd.

HERE LYES
JAMES AND ROBERT
DUNS, THOMAS AND
JOHN STEVENSONS,
JAMES McCLIVE,
ANDREU McCALL, WHO
WERE SURPRISED
AT PRAYER IN HIS
HOUSE, BY COLNELL
DOUGLAS, LIEVTNAN
LIVINGSTON, AND

CORNET
JAMES DOUGLAS AND
BY TEM MOST IMPIOUS
LY AND CRUELLY
MURTERED FOR TEIR
ADHERENCE TO SCOT
LANDS REFORMATION
COVENANTS NATIONAL
AND SOLEMN LEAGUE
1685

LOCH TROOL

Quiet the water
Gentle the sun
Greens, blues, purples chase
Across the shale and granite hills
Whose tormented creation
Is but an unemotive line
In our geology,
Past convulsions
Presenting us
With peace and beauty.
Here black waters mirror the blue sky;
There they sparkle
Brightness given for brightness received.

Quiet the six-fold grave
Buried principles
Reminding the present
Of stands still to be taken,
To the hills they lifted their eyes
Whence came no aid,
Their covenant the worth of each
The testimony all possess,
For that the martyrdom
The green wood stained with red,
And now the near-forgotten monument
Marking a finer cause than does the kingly stone
To which some pay the greater honour.

May quietness be preserved
For all.
A healing thing.

Arthur Clegg

CONTENTS

GAZETTEER

INTRODUCTION

Welcome to South-west Scotland!

In many ways this is a lost and forgotten area, an area of wild and weird beauty, a lonely area.   Yet, with an incomparable variety of coast and hill, town and village, sea and hill loch, ancient and modern, it is surely the ideal holiday area.   More accessible than the Highlands, it has much Highland scenery, a warmer climate and lower rainfall.   The hills and forests contain a wide range of wild life; the light and reflections on the Solway coast have long been irresistible to artists; ancient chapels, abbeys and castles bring history to vivid life.   The towns, especially on the coast, have everything possible in the way of entertainments.   In sum, a superb holiday area.

But this book is not designed to attract you here, for you are here already!   It is meant, instead, to suggest how you can get the best out of your stay.

Inevitably, it pre-supposes that you travel by car.   There is no other way of getting about these days.   It was different in the not-so-distant past, but now public transport, except along the coastal strip, is virtually non-existent.   Fortunately, there is a most excellent network of roads, and, more fortunate still, they are never really busy, even in the height of the holiday season.

There is a series of suggested tours in this book.   Perhaps these are not really necessary, for wherever you go, you will surely find places of great beauty and interest.   However, the suggested tours *ensure* that you will miss but little during a holiday here.

Of course, this is a large area to cover. Therefore there are two sets of suggested tours, one starting at Ayr in the north, and the other at Castle Douglas in the south. They are all circular tours, though, and thus can be joined at any point. There is no particular reason for starting the tours at Ayr and Castle Douglas, except that tours must start *somewhere,* and those two delightful towns are as good as anywhere else. But if you are staying in Stranraer, or Dumfries, or Girvan, or anywhere else in the area, you will still find the suggestions useful: you merely join the tours at a different point. Perhaps ideally, to really make the best of a holiday in South-west Scotland, one should have what the tourist industry calls a 'two-centre holiday', that is, stay for a while in one place, then move to another.

However, no roads, and thus no suggested tours go into the real heart of the hills; the lovely and secret places demand that you visit them on foot.

Coming from the south, you hardly know that you have crossed a border into Scotland, and certainly there is nothing now to remind you of the bitterness of the past, when these border lands were fought over repeatedly down the centuries. Only the lovely old Border Ballads, beloved of every folk singer, are there to remind us. Those, and a host of castles, fortified houses and towers.

But perhaps the very emptiness of the land should alert us to the fact that this is a unique area. For hundreds of years this land on both sides of the Solway Firth was the scene of incessant battle and slaughter, nation against nation, family against family. While England and Scotland struggled bloodily over the centuries, each repeatedly burning, killing and plundering over the land, the people took to the hills, living as best they could, and dying when they must. As the great battles of nations passed into history, the people emerged, dazed and anachronistic, for they knew not the ways of peace, only the ways of war and pillage. So the struggles continued, with each family — Armstrongs, Douglasses, Grahams,

Maxwells and many more — engaged in furious and endless raids on cattle, land and wealth. Some flourished, but many died, and the land was desolate and empty.

Those days are past, but the memories remain. And the land is still empty and quiet, but lovely with a beauty hard to express, particularly if the visitor is aware of a bitter history.

However British they might be, the Scots do see themselves as being different from the rest of the British people. Wherever they are, and however long settled in foreign parts, they retain an essential Scottishness and pride. This is reflected in the existence of innumerable Burns Clubs, St. Andrew's Societies, Caledonian Clubs and Clan Societies throughout the world, and this nostalgia, it seems, is an inherited thing, for, far from dying out, these associations of expatriate Scots go on from strength to strength.

It must be remembered that, in the long and bitter struggle to retain national independence from England, Scotland was never conquered. It became part of the United Kingdom in 1707, but that was by Treaty, not by force of arms, and even today many Scots regard that Treaty as an act of abysmal treachery, perpetrated by venal leaders for their own profit. *'We are bought and sold with England's gold. Sic a parcel of rogues in a nation,'* as the ballad puts it.

Perhaps the first real figure to appear out of the mists of secular history in the dark ages of Scotland was King Kennneth Mac-Alpin. In 844 A.D. he united the Scots and the Picts under his own leadership and successfully defended their territory against all the many roving hordes of central European tribes which wandered the land in those days. This unity was shattered in 1069 when King Malcolm III married a Saxon, Margaret, a woman of rare strong will, who broke up the Celtic church, imposed feudal systems of landholding, and the use of English and French as court languages.

Gradually, over 200 years, the English influence grew, and finally, by marriage, the English crown had a reasonable claim on the Scottish throne.   But this was too much even for the vacillating King John Balliol, and in 1296 the English invaded under Edward I — whom the English know as 'The Hammer of the Scots', and the Scots as something quite different.   It was out of this struggle that William Wallace arose as a great leader, and after him Robert Bruce, who succeeded where Wallace gloriously failed.   Robert Bruce welded his nation into a unity so strong that it defeated the English and lasted for 400 years.

Out of the victory of Bruce came the *'Declaration of Arbroath'*, a great, ringing statement which comes down the centuries.

'For as long as one hundred of us shall remain alive we shall never in any wise submit to the rule of the English, for it is not for glory alone we fight, for riches, or for honours, but for freedom, which no good man loses but with his life.'

And so it was for 400 years, until the noble sentiments of Arbroath drowned in the inflow of gold and trade.

But enough of the past, although a little understanding of the country's history can only add to your pleasures in the present. And there is more to come in this Introduction to South West Scotland!

Because you are in Scotland, you can go on foot where you will, for Scottish law does not recognise the idea of trespass.   Naturally, you do not damage hedges, fences or crops, and if you do, may find yourself liable.   And should you be carrying a fishing rod or a gun, that is a different kettle of fish (or dish of venison stew), for then you might be guilty of trespassing in pursuit of game.

Wherever you go in South-west Scotland, you cannot easily escape the past, for it is all around you, and the deep, ice-gouged valleys have supported man for 10,000 years, from the Old Stone Age onwards.   This was the land of the Galwyddel (*Welsh:*

Stranger Gaels), and they left faint clues for us to wonder at—age old stones, burial cairns and forts, relics of ancient religions and forgotten battles. They left us one of our names, too, for 'Galloway' is derived from *Galwyddel.*

Even today, there is a sense of isolation from the rest of Britain, and that has always been so. Warring clans, religious strife, agricultural revolution, gypsies, coastal raiders and smugglers have left us a wealth of historical associations, with a wonderful and diverse heritage of buildings and sites. The whole area is bestrewn with pre-historic monuments, Roman forts, Dark Age religious remains, splendid medieval abbeys, castles and towerhouses, old farms, old mills. And every village (and most towns) seems to be newly scrubbed and painted, and throughout the summer newly decorated with the brightest of flowers.

It is perfectly possible in one day to pass from looking at mysterious, prehistoric "cup and ring" marks, to 4th and 5th century crosses at Whithorn and Kirkmadrine, to the medieval wonders of Glenluce, to the ferocious self-sufficiency of feudal Threave Castle, to the civilised beauty of the Age of Enlightenment at Culzean Castle, to the early industrial remains of mills and iron foundries, and finally to the finest of modern sculpture by Rodin, Moore and Epstein at the wonderful moorland gallery of Shawhead, near Castle Douglas. And all that in one day: a microcosm of history! Indeed, what a place for a holiday!

Of course, you cannot hope to explore it all. Nor, perhaps should you even try. This book, though, will lead you to the best of a very wonderful feast: eat what you will of it today, and return again — and again — for further helpings.

You will find that one of the benefits of the Forestry Commission is that they have driven rough but quite passable roads deep into the hills. These are not marked on maps. They are often closed, but permission to travel them can usually be obtained from the local Forester. Do seek such permission, though. Otherwise you

5

may find yourself having to reverse half a mile down a mountain with a large and impatient timber lorry nuzzling at your bonnet. If that happens, you might learn some words of the old Scots Doric tongue that do not appear in the dictionaries! But, with permission, those forest roads will take you deeper and further into the wildness than you have ever imagined. You will be able to see aspects of the hills not possible from the roads.

For the walker, too, these roads are a great blessing: you can go dry-shod to places once known only to shepherds and their flocks. Be careful, though, for there is a peculiar will o' the wisp quality about those tracks, a constant feeling that you must see round the next shoulder, climb the next hill.

And on the vast moors, as you walk or ride, there is also a sense of strangeness, a sense that somehow those who once strode these hills, and also loved them and lived in them, are still with you.

There are:—

'Grey recumbent tombs of the dead in desert places,
Standing stones on the vacant wine-red moor.'

The people of South-west Scotland have long been stubborn, born of a stubborn country. This was Covenanting Country, and almost every churchyard has a grave or two of those most stubborn people, who, rather than accept into their religion what they disliked, would *'allow the winds to make whistles of their bones'.* There have not been many Catholic martyrs for the Latin ritual, nor Church of England martyrs for the King James's Version!

Even Shakespeare knew of Galloway, its character and its characters. *'Knew we not Galloway nags?'* asks Pistol in Henry IV, and he was not talking about horses! Incidentally, the English certainly did know about Galloway horses, for Robert Bruce rode one — especially at Bannockburn.

This stubbornness — and courage — is shown in the legend of

Trost of the Long Knife.   He, his father and his brother were the last of their tribe to know the secret of brewing Heather Ale.   (In those happy days, Heather Ale was the drink to bring glory, strength, courage and many another good thing.)   The three of them were captured by Niall of the Nine Hostages, who was determined to get the secret of Heather Ale for himself, as who wouldn't be.   Trost offered to give away the secret, telling Niall that first his father and his brother must be thrown off a nearby and convenient cliff, lest they punish his treachery.   Niall was happy to do this — he would probably have done it anyway — and then Trost himself leaped off the cliff to his death, taking with him that great secret, to the loss and detriment of everyone ever since.

Being so close to Ireland, and easily visible from there, these lands early attracted wandering tribes.   It was easier to make the short sea crossing from Ireland than to cross the treacherous Solway Firth.   The first wanderers seem to have congregated around Luce Bay, and have left us flint knives and arrowheads, as well as whale bones and deer antlers, in their middens.   By and large, those people, the people of the Old Stone Age, stayed on the shores and in the river valleys, for they could not conquer the great hills clad in oak and Scots Pine.   Their implements were inadequate for that.

The people of the New Stone Age were farmers, rather than hunters.   They, too, could not tackle the great trees, and most of their homesteads were high in the hills, where trees did not grow.   They had domesticated cattle and sheep, and grew corn. Their dead, or at least their dead leaders, were buried in great cairns, stone chambers covered by a mound of earth.   The finest, perhaps, is White Cairn, near Glen Trool.

The mastery of metal, first bronze, then iron, was a revolutionary change.   The Celtic peoples from central Europe mastered these new techniques, and consequently were able to travel far and fast, imposing their will on others.   From about 5000 B.C. those strangers, warriors and craftsmen, spread into South-west Scotland.

The tribes had various names, and cannot easily be distinguished one from the other, but there were Picts, Scots, and Britons. Those who reached South-west Scotland, though, were known as Gaels, and their Gaelic language survived here until 300 years ago and less. Indeed, it survives today, in the beautiful names of the hills and fells. It should be remembered that these Picts and Scots and Gaels were far from being the uncivilised, uncultured barbarians they are usually represented as being. Far indeed from that. They had a highly organised society, and a surprisingly democratic one. They had a culture which even today we can only wonder about. Their designs and patterns, cut deep into hard stone, are beautiful and intricate — so intricate, indeed, that many of them even today can only be copied, not projected, for the mathematics of them cannot be understood. The border round the cover of this book is one such Celtic pattern, probably Pictish in origin.

The chief monument of the Iron Age is the hill fort, a whole township set on a hill and surrounded by a wall. It defended a whole area, for probably the cattle and sheep and the weaker people withdrew from all round about to the shelter of the fort whenever attack threatened, and the able-bodied defended the walls.

Sometimes *crannogs* were built instead of hill forts, and those were more easily defensible. They were forts built on an island of logs set in a loch, and approached by one narrow track over the water. Often, that track was submerged, and zigged and zagged in a way known only to the local people. Perhaps the best, within the area covered by this book, is that at Castle Douglas itself.

After the Gaels came the Romans, in the first century A.D. Although north of Hadrian's Wall, the Romans did maintain a military presence in Galloway, probably to prevent the turbulent Gallovidians from crossing the Solway and attacking the Romans from the rear, behind their Maginot Line.

It was during the Roman occupation that Christianity first came to Scotland. St. Ninian, a native missionary bishop, set up his tiny chapel of *Candida Casa,* the White House, at Whithorn.

After the Romans left, the Gaels faced attack from the Strathclyde Britons, and so, after the Roman pattern, they built a great stone and turf rampart from Stranraer to Dumfries. That they could undertake such a task, and organise it, shows that they must have had a considerable amount of civilisation and government. Traces of this great rampart, the De'il's Dyke, can still be seen here and there, particularly around Glen Trool, and further north, around Sanquhar.

About 300 years of (comparative) peace followed, until the Picts and Scots broke through the wall. They were driven back, though, and a lot of their own territory annexed. About 800 A.D., the long-ships of the Vikings appeared, and coming from the sea, they were behind the wall, and soon managed to overthrow the old regime. For a full 300 years they were overlords of South-west Scotland. They left little trace, however, except for a number of names, like all the many 'fells'. (*Norse: Fjell,* a mountain) and the river Fleet, (*Norse: Fljot,* a river). What they did leave were a lot of heroic tales, peopled by great men with great names, like Thorfinn the Skull-Cleaver, and Sigurd the Stout. One would give much to meet with *them* in Valhalla, over a barrel of Heather Ale!

Gradually, after the Norman conquest of England, Norman feudalism spread into Scotland, but even more gradually into this turbulent area. But it did happen, and a whole string of great castles and forts was built to enforce it. Loch Doon Castle, Garlies Castle near Newton Stewart, and Castle Stewart itself, are examples of those feudal strongholds.

The Scots, however, never really acknowledged the over-lordship of the English feudal kings, and in 1292 a Galloway baron, John Balliol, was proclaimed King of Scotland. He was not much of a king, though, and in 1296 he surrendered his kingdom to Edward I of England.

That pleased few and angered many. Amongst the many was Robert Bruce, Earl of Carrick, just north-west of Galloway. By somewhat dubious means, Robert was proclaimed King of Scotland, and promptly retired to Ireland. There he gathered his men, and with a few hundred followers landed near his castle of Turnberry in 1307. By a brilliant guerilla war, culminating in the great set-piece battle of Bannockburn in 1314, Scotland's independence was regained.

Although by no means without incident or interest, the next 250 years were fairly peaceable in South-west Scotland — at least by previous standards. Troubles came, though, with an attempt by King James VI of Scotland to impose Bishops on the Scottish Church, to bring them into line with the English Church. The Reformation was not long past, and that was a time of suffering. Most people seemed to see the imposition of Bishops as the beginning of a return to the Roman Church. Perhaps significantly, most of the vast landholdings of the Catholic establishment had passed into the hands of the great nobles: they most certainly had no intention of allowing even the shadow of Rome to return.

The struggle continued through the reigns of James VI, Charles I and Charles II. The Solemn League and Covenant, signed by the Presbyterian leaders in 1639, totally disavowed Bishops and all their works, and the Coventanters, and especially the men of South-west Scotland, fought well and expensively for Parliament against the King in the Civil War. They expected Cromwell to confirm their own form of church.

On the restoration of the monarchy in 1661, Charles II again appointed Bishops to govern the Scottish Church. Then began 'The Killing Time'. The Covenanters, stubborn as Gallovidians ever were, refused to accept the Bishops: the Government in London insisted that they did.

A 'Highland Host' — an army of mercenary soldiers who had to live off the land — was brought south to enforce the Government's will, and by its looting and indiscriminate cruelty left scars visible to this day.   After enduring the horrors of the Highland Host, the South-west of Scotland gave but little support or encouragement to Prince Charles Edward and his Jacobite Highlanders in the 1745 uprising.

The Government troops stayed after the Highland Host left, and there were many more deaths still to come and much suffering. Only after the death of Charles II and the enthronement of William and Mary in 1688 did peace return.   The Presbyterian Church, without Bishops, was recognised as the established religion of Scotland.   But by then, Scotland, and in particular the South-west, had been greatly impoverished by the troubles.

But tranquillity did not long endure.   The local landowners saw the opportunity of increasing the profits from their vast holdings. With the Union of Parliaments in 1707, the great market of England was opened to Scottish producers of meat, and, to produce cattle and sheep effectively, the old farming system, with its mass of almost self-sufficient peasants, had to be destroyed, and the peasants along with the system.

Permanent dykes and hedges were put up to enclose parks, and the leases of smallholdings ended.   Not surprisingly, the peasants resisted, and bands of 'Levellers' destroyed hedges and dykes almost as quickly as the lairds raised them.   Troops and dragoons again ranged over the moors, and the Levellers were hunted like their Covenanting fathers (and mothers) before them.

One of the leaders of the Levellers was Billy Marshal, King of the Gypsies.   He had been a soldier, and brought military discipline to the previously disorderly rabble.   Arming his men with long iron spikes, Billy Marshall and his band were able to overturn long lengths of dyke, much more quickly than the enclosers could put them up.   As the poet wrote:

Against the poor the lairds prevail,
With all their wicked works,
Who will enclose both hill and dale
And turn cornfields to parks.
The lords and lairds they drive us out,
From mailings where we dwell,
The poor man cries "Where shall we go?"
The rich say "Go to Hell!".

Billy Marshall, incidentally, must have been a most remarkable character. He died at the age of 120, having sired several children after his centenary, and there are stories of great battles between his gypsies and the bands of tinkers who also roamed the roads of Galloway and Ayrshire.

Of course, the lands were finally enclosed, and the peasant farmers moved into new villages and trained as weavers, mostly, to satisfy the great American market, also newly opened to Scotland by the Act of Union.

The new 'improved' farms were large, and some workers were still employed, of course, and a hard life they had of it. That brilliant but strangely neglected Scottish writer James Barke, gives a vivid description of that hard life in his moving novel *The Land of the Leal.*

A hundred years later, in the early 19th. century, the lovely black Galloway cattle were replaced by black-faced sheep on most of the hills. And that is almost the last change to have taken place in the countryside of South-west Scotland. On the lower lands, the brown and white Ayrshire cattle, which are every childs' vision of a cow, have been replaced by the black and white Friesian dairy cow, and on some of the hills the sheep now overwinter on great expanses of turnips.

Occasionally you will still see that most charming of cows, the Belted Galloway, with its white cummerbund showing off its glossy black hide.

The other great visible change, of course, is the plantations of the Forestry Commission. These have spread far and wide over the hills in the past fifty years, and the debate about them shows no sign of ending.

Beyond question, they provide some employment in an area where there is otherwise none. Beyond question, too, they at least produce *something* from land that otherwise would produce only the occasional sheep. No-one today would work those uplands as small farms, as our fore-fathers did, and suffer and toil as they did. Only those with no knowledge of it can be sentimental about the past. If the Forestry Commission was not there, the hillsides would perhaps be even more natural and beautiful, but it would be a sterile beauty. It would be a long step towards driving even more people from this land, and leaving it as nothing but a lovely and empty playground. However, in thinking about the work of the Forestry Commission, it must always be remembered that the changes it has wrought on the land are almost certainly *permanent* changes. It is unlikely that that land will ever again carry any crop other than trees.

Even today, this is a *very* empty area. Apart from a very few towns, mainly along the coast, the only other populated places are small villages. The narrow, fertile coastal strip is intensively farmed, but the rest is bare hill and moor, cut through by rich and lovely valleys.

Red deer roam over the hills, and some of the mature forests. At the turn of the year, the roaring of stags, as they mark their territory and claim their mates, echoes up most of the valleys. It comes even before the snowdrops, as a herald of the spring still to come.

Nor are deer the only animals living on these hills. In fact, there is a variety perhaps unmatched in Britain. There are wild uplands, and the fauna and flora typical of the Highlands, but the area has a mild climate, and thus there are also many Lowland species. (It was said recently that this area has no climate — only samples of weather.　But that was a jaundiced view.)

In the great de-afforestation process that took place 200 years ago during the Agricultural Revolution, many of the woodland species — pine martens and so on — vanished from South-west Scotland, and were replaced by the creatures of the moorland — blue hare, grouse, plover and merlin.　Red deer adapted to the change, and survived, as in much of Scotland.

Today, as re-afforestation spreads, there is again much change, and it is difficult to foresee the fauna our children may be watching.　Today, though, a sharp eye might see both red and roe deer, foxes, mountain and brown hares and otters.　And mink, which are destroyed on sight.

On Benyallery (Gaelic: *Beinn Iolaire*—Hill of Eagles) golden eagles still nest, and presumably have done so ever since our Gaelic-speaking ancestors roamed and named the hills.

There are also buzzards, which at a distance are often mistaken for eagles.　Other predatory birds often sighted are the peregrine falcon, a haunter of the crags, and the merlin, usually hunting over the heather hills.　Lower down, there are sparrow hawks, kestrels and hen harriers, although perhaps only the kestrel is common.

The vicious hooded crow, enemy of all shepherds, is not normally found in these lands, although there are many carrion crows, and quite often ravens.

The tawny, the short-eared, the long-eared and the barn owl are all quite common, and will probably increase as the conifer plantations mature.

Perhaps, though, the best-loved upland bird is the curlew.　No moorland walk, surely, would be complete without the accompaniment of its friendly and evocative call, and fortunately there are lots of curlews in this area, and lots of green plover, although the golden plover is somewhat less plentiful.

Of course, as well as birds of the uplands, there are vast numbers

14

of wild fowl, on the Solway coast especially, but also on a number of inland lochs. There are barnacle geese in the Caerlaverock Nature Reserve, as well as considerable flocks of other geese and wildfowl. Greylag geese breed hereabouts, and both pink-footed and white-fronted geese are common visitors.

Shovellers, teal, mallard and tufted duck all breed on local lochs, and there are some notable heronries.

For those interested in sea birds, this area is of uncommon interest. Terns and cormorants, black guillemots, kittiwake and fulmar all breed on these coasts, cliffs and islands, and there is a wide range of gulls — common, herring, black headed, greater and lesser black backed.

This is, of course, above all the land of Robert Burns. In his own day, Burns was the poet of the people. Peasants, weavers, servant girls, school teachers, lawyers and lairds all bought his books, and read them. Today, most people, even here in his own country, do not read his works, and know only a few odd lines — and those often wrong! This is a great pity. Burns is just as relevant, and his work just as beautiful, today as two hundred years ago. It is *not* difficult to read or understand — certainly no more difficult than Shakespeare and much less than Milton. Of course, even the Scot of today has to struggle a little with the language of those poems written in the Scots tongue. But the struggle is very much worth while. And every collection of his works today contains a glossary of the Scots words. Besides, Burns also wrote most beautiful English. *'The Bonny Lass o' Ballochmyle'* is English very pure and delightful: so are many others.

It would add much delight to your holiday if you bought a collection of Burns's poems, and read them as you visit the places he wrote about.

A word about maps. The little map in this booklet is designed only to show the roads used in these tours, and nothing else. For a serious walker, only the Ordnance Survey maps will do. Of course (and it *always* happens like this!), you need two of them to cover the area. Perhaps the best and most generally useful map is the Geographia 3 miles to 1 inch map of South-west Scotland. The A.A. distributes this to its members, but most bookshops also stock it.

The Gazetteer in this book is as complete as possible, but not every place of interest and beauty has a separate entry: it would become unwieldy if that were so. In fact, most Gazetteer entries contain information about things and places close by, or associated with, the Gazetteer entry itself. Actually, it is best, as with all guide books, to not treat it simply as a work of reference, just to look up information on wherever you happen to be, but rather read it right through. In that way, you will able to savour the whole area, and better appreciate the details of the big picture.

So, again, welcome to South-west Scotland, and may you have a very fine holiday.

WHAT TO DO ON A FINE DAY

Of course, this whole book is designed to tell you about enjoyable things to do on days both wet and fine. With luck, there will be some days when the weather is so fine that you really do not want to be on the road, even to visit such delightful places as those described in this book.

Those are the days for lying on a beach, soaking up sun and sea water, beachcombing, perhaps scrambling over rocks and watching the miniature world of the rock pools.

South-west Scotland is rich in beaches. Kippford, Monreith, most of Luce Bay and long stretches of the Mull of Galloway coast are ideal for such pleasures as beaches give. Generally, the Atlantic coast, from the Mull of Galloway itself to Ayr, is more rocky — although certainly well enough endowed with excellent beaches, for example at Girvan and at Ayr itself. On that coast, though, the best fun is exploring caves, and there are many of them. Culzean Castle has perhaps the best, but there are many others, at Turnberry, for example. Further south, by Bennane Head, is Sawney Bean's cave, if you dare to enter it!

A wonderful way to spend a fine day is to go for a sail on the paddle steamer 'Waverley'. She is the last sea-going paddle steamer in Britain, and is beautiful. She sails regularly up and down the Ayrshire coast, with trips to Arran, round Ailsa Craig and over to Kintyre. She is a fine old lady, and all her inner workings, the engines and paddles are open to view. It could be that your mother and *her* mother took their pleasure on such a trip, and sailing in her today is a fine exercise in nostalgia.

Visiting the many lovely gardens of South-west Scotland could take up a whole holiday, and there are worse ways than that to spend a holiday. Threave, Castle Kennedy, Port Logan and Bargany could in fact each occupy a day, and you still would not have seen everything. The parks of Ayr are invariably a rainbow of colour, but might well make you green with envy that you cannot get the same effects in your garden.

Golf, of course, is everywhere, and there is a choice of everything from village putting greens to the international standards of Troon and Turnberry. As an added dividend, many of the courses provide most excellent views, as well as some healthy exercise.

This corner of Scotland is also a stronghold of bowling, and there are greens in nearly every village. Competition is very keen, and the standard of play high.

The nature reserve at Caerlaverock is for birdwatchers, and the range of waterfowl, as well as land birds, is quite extraordinary. But you can birdwatch without going to Caerlaverock. Every hill carries its bird population, and there are some remarkable rarities.

Sea-angling, either from boats or off the beaches, is available pretty well everywhere along the coast. There are fine catches every season, and the local boat skippers seem to be highly skilled at finding fish, either game fish or fish for the pan. Tackle is often provided by the boat skippers, but take your own 'refreshment' along, either to toast success, or drown regret.

For the angler, this area is paradise (or, sometimes, purgatory). There are salmon and sea trout in the rivers, and trout in both rivers and lochs. Virtually all the fishing is private, in the sense that you must buy a ticket, but tickets are certainly not expensive, and great sport can be had. The Forestry Commission has stocked and maintains some notable lochs. Tickets, usually, from the local hotels, tackle shops or Forestry Offices.

Above all, this is the country for walking. You can do everything from strolling along the prom. at Ayr to a circuit of the summits of the Galloway Hills. And that really *is* a feat. For some of the best walks, consult the leaflets issued by the Forestry Commission. But, please, when walking, close gates behind you, do not break down hedges or fences, be very careful with matches and fire, and, above all, keep your dog under control. Really, only walking can take you to the finest and most lovely places. You can go by car to Loch Doon, for example, and very fine it is, but only your feet can take you to Loch Enoch, remote in the hills, and lovely with its granite sand beaches and the strange little loch on an island in the loch itself.

Wanlockhead Lead Mines Museum is probably best visited on a fine day, because much of the most interesting material is outside. But, wet or fine, it really is a place very well well worth seeing.

WHAT TO DO ON A WET DAY

It has to be admitted that there are occasional wet days in Scotland, even in the summer.   For the holiday maker, though, a wet day need not be a lost day.   There are many entertaining, enjoyable and even instructive ways to spend a wet day in South-west Scotland — and that is not including the possibilities of staying in bed or in the local bar.

A fairly recent development in this area is the establishment of a number of small local museums.   Most of these are private ventures, not funded by the government in any way.   They are extremely interesting.   It is difficult to make a recommendation here, but there are particularly fine examples in Newton Stewart and Kirkcudbright.

The little Tam o' Shanter museum in Ayr is delightful.   It still resembles very closely the inn it used to be, from where Tam began his midnight ride, and if you want to learn more about Robert Burns, then talk to the Curator: he knows *everything*.   Unfortunately, the museum is so tiny that it won't occupy you for the whole of a wet day — perhaps only for a shower.

The Stewartry Museum in Kirkcudbright tries hard, and generally succeeds, in presenting a potted history of that strange and turbulent area.   Broughton House is also in Kirkcudbright, and the library there, and the works of art, are a delight, and show how the beauty of the Solway worked on the mind of a very competent artist.

Right out in the country, at New Abbey (Sweetheart Abbey), is the very unusual little Shambellie House Museum of Costume. Two centuries of what passed for fashionable European dress are on display there, and most interesting it all is.

Further north again, the Burns Centre at Alloway tries very hard, and with some success, to present an honest picture of Robert Burns and his times. You don't have to be a Burns enthusiast (although everyone *should* be!) to enjoy this centre and its 'audio-visual display'.

Perhaps you like swimming. Ayr baths are rather special. As well as a 25 metre pool, there are diving and learners' pools. But there is also a sauna, Turkish baths and a thing called an 'Aerotone Bath' — which sounds like something a Middle Eastern Oil Mogul might have in his private jet. If all that is not enough, there is also a conditioning room and a gymnasium. And, to allow recovery from it all, there is a lounge with T.V. Probably, in fact, you could spend your whole holiday in those swimming baths, and go home both fit and very clean.

Strangely, few of the Stately Homes of this area are open to the public. The lairds have not imitated the lords. However, Drumlanrig Castle, near Dumfries, is an exception, and very much worth a visit. It is hard to say whether you should go there on a wet day or a fine day. If it is wet, you could happily spend hours looking over the fine and beautiful interior: if it is fine, walking the woods and gardens is always a joy.

Culzean Castle, near Ayr, can also certainly occupy a full day, wet or fine, and very enjoyably too. It is most beautifully restored and maintained by the National Trust. Of course, you pay to enter, but it is money very well spent. Perhaps it would be even better if you joined the Trust and visited other properties.

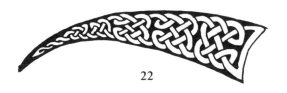

TOURS

Every visitor to South-west Scotland is certainly going to visit the obvious places, such as Kirkcudbright, Alloway, Dumfries, Ayr and the Mull of Galloway. All the obvious places, and a lot of the not so obvious, are described in detail in the Gazetteer of this book. However, this area is blessed with a very remarkable network of minor roads, most of them running through very beautiful countryside, and passing lovely sights. These suggested Tours try to stick to minor roads—some of them very minor indeed. You will find them very quiet, even in summer.

A nice mixture of the main roads to the principal holiday attractions, and leisurely travel along minor roads for the sheer joy of them, will help to give you a holiday to remember.

It must be admitted that some of the Tours cover a considerable mileage—more, perhaps, than can comfortably be covered in one day. This would seem like an admirable reason for having what the Tourist Industry calls a "Two-Centre Holiday". That is, stay part of the time in one place, then move on for the remainder of your holiday to another centre.

However, in fact all the Tours *can* be done in one day, thanks to a fine road network. And most of them are designed so that you can cut out any part that doesn't seem very attractive to you. If you do that, though, you will miss some unusual pleasures.

TOURS STARTING AT CASTLE DOUGLAS

TOUR ONE
Castle Douglas to Gelston (B736), Sheillahill (B727), Auchencairn (unclassified), Kirkcudbright (A711), Tongland (A762), Castle Douglas (unclassified, turn right in Tongland.)

This is a tour for the wanderer. Don't stick to the main suggested road, but meander down the lanes. You have to retrace your steps from some places, like Abbey Burnfoot and Balcarry Point, but surely you will enjoy every yard of the road. It is very much worth while to arrange to visit the remarkable Tongland hydro-electric generating station near Kirkcudbright. No noise, no smell, no smoke, no radiation: just lots of very cheap power. See salmon climbing ladders there, as they go up river to spawn.

Refer to Gazetteer for information on: Castle Douglas, Kirkcudbright, Beeswing.

TOUR TWO
Castle Douglas to Dalbeattie (A745), Kippford (A710), Sandyhills (A710), Kirkbean (A710), New Abbey (for Sweetheart Abbey), Dumfries, Drumsleet (A711), Lochfoot (unclassified), Milton, Haugh of Urr (for Mote of Urr), Castle Douglas.

Great stretches of unpolluted sandy beaches on this tour, and a lot of sailing. And whatever you miss out, you must visit Sweetheart Abbey. There is great walking around there. Also look at, and wonder about, the massive, mysterious Mote of Urr.

Refer to Gazetteer for information on: Castle Douglas, Sweetheart Abbey, Dumfries.

TOUR THREE
Castle Douglas to New Galloway (A713), Newton Stewart (A712), Creetown (A75), Culcranchie (unclassified; turn left in Creetown), Upper Rusko and Rusko Castle, Anwoth, Gatehouse of Fleet (A75), Low Barlay (unclassified, but branch right at village), Laurieston and Bellymack (!), Castle Douglas (A75).

This tour takes you right through the stupendous Galloway Forest Park, and there is no finer road in Scotland. The unclassified road from Creetown to Gatehouse of Fleet runs over high and wild country and is a perpetual delight.

Refer to Gazetteer for information on: Castle Douglas, New Galloway, Minigaff, Newton Stewart, Balmaclellan, Creetown, Gatehouse of Fleet.

TOUR FOUR
Castle Douglas to Newton Stewart (A75), Wigtown (A714), Glenluce, Newton Stewart (A75), New Galloway (A712), Laurieston (A762), Ringford (A762), Castle Douglas (A75).

Another tour for the wanderer. However, wanderer or not, you *must* visit the Whithorn peninsula. By keeping the sea on your left all the way, you will go through Kirkmadrine, Monreith, Port William, and eventually Glenluce. That way, too, you will go through such delightful villages as Braehead, and Kirkinner. Really, though, you should not go *through* them, but stop there. Tiny lanes run down to the sheltered water and beaches of Wigtown Bay from those villages. There are great stretches of empty sands. There is a strangeness about the beauties of the Whithorn peninsula, a strangeness perhaps unique in Scotland. It is difficult to describe just what it is — you really must experience it for yourself. And don't worry if you think you are lost in the maze of country roads: eventually you will reach the sea. It is also suggested that you return from Newton Stewart through the

Galloway Forest Park. That road, in the reverse direction, was also covered in Tour Three, but you will be astonished at how different it is travelling in the other direction. Those great hills never look the same on two successive days.

Refer to Gazetteer for information on: Castle Douglas, Newton Stewart, Glenluce, Whithorn.

TOUR FIVE

Castle Douglas to St. John's Town of Dalry (A713), Carsphairn (B7000 & B729), [by Kendoon Loch], Dalmellington (A713) [but divert to the left at Mossdale, and go to Loch Doon], Straiton (B741), Newton Stewart (Unclassified), Castle Douglas (A75).

This tour takes you through very beautiful, very wild, country; it is a mountain road of the finest quality. Whatever you miss, do not miss Loch Trool. A visit there could be the high point of your holiday.

Refer to Gazetteer for information on: Castle Douglas, St. John's Town of Dalry, Straiton, Newton Stewart, Minigaff, Glen Trool.

TOUR SIX

Castle Douglas to Stranraer (A75), Mull of Galloway (A716), Stranraer, Castle Douglas (A75).

There is so much to enjoy in the Mull of Galloway that it is suggested you keep to the main road, (A75) which is quite fast (but also very attractive), to get there more quickly. Do not though, try to resist the temptations of Castle Kennedy and Glenluce. Wander round the Mull of Galloway, where *everything* is worth looking at. Allow yourself to be seduced by the beauty of it all. Then, perhaps, go straight back to your hotel or caravan and digest what you have absorbed in a most memorable day.

Refer to Gazetteer for information on: Castle Douglas, Gatehouse of Fleet, Creetown, Newton Stewart, Glenluce, Castle Kennedy, Stranraer, Port Logan, Mull of Galloway.

26

TOUR SEVEN

Castle Douglas to Dumfries (A75), Moniaive (A76 & B729),
Thornhill (A7027), Mennock (A76), Leadhills (B797), Elvan-
foot (B7040), Fingland (A702), Thornhill, Moniaive (A702),
St. John's Town of Dalry (A702), Castle Douglas (A713).

This very interesting tour takes you by miniature Highland
Glens and Passes to the Lead Mines Museum at Wanlockhead. Earlier, the Bonny Annie Laurie country is traversed, and
you really cannot pass Drumlanrig Castle without visiting it and
the wonderful grounds surrounding it. St. John's Town of Dalry
is most attractive, with grand views, and the return to Castle
Douglas is down the length of Loch Ken.

Refer to Gazetteer for information on: Castle Douglas, Dumfries, Wanlockhead, St. John's Town of Dalry.

TOURS STARTING AT AYR

TOUR EIGHT

Ayr to Dunure (A719),Maidens, Turnberry, Girvan (A77),
Dailly (B741), Straiton, Dalmellington, Patna (A713), Ayr.

The first part of this tour is down the coast, with fine, sandy
beaches, rocks for pools and scrambling over, and thrilling
caves.   Culzean is quite simply a 'must', and so is Dunure. Later,
there is a fine run over high moorland and finally a glimpse of an old
coal mining and iron working town,with interesting relics of the
recent past, and some rich farmlands.

Refer to Gazetteer for information on: Ayr, Dunure, Girvan,
Ailsa Craig, Straiton, Dalmellington.

TOUR NINE

Ayr to Alloway (B7024), Maybole via Brown Carrick Hill
(A719 and unclassified), Crosshill, North Balloch, Nick o' the
Balloch, Straiton, Kirkmichael (B7045), Dalrymple (Unclass-
ified), Ayr (A713).

Alloway is the very heart of the Land o' Burns, and cannot be
missed.   Brown Carrick Hill has wonderful views, unmatched of
their kind in Southern Scotland.   After that the route takes you
over high and wild country before droppping down to dairy farms
and the road to Ayr.

Refer to Gazetteer for information on: Alloway, Brown Carrick
Hill, Balloch, Straiton, Kirkmichael.

TOUR TEN
Ayr to Maybole (A77), Kirkoswald, Girvan, Ballantrae, Col-
monell (A765), Pinwherry, Barr (B734), Old Dailly, Crosshill
(B7027), Minishant (B734), Ayr (A77).

The road passes two very interesting ruins, Baltersan Castle and
Crossraguel Abbey: both are right on the road, and well worth a
visit.   Ballantrae is the place to see salmon in the river.   The
Stinchar valley is singularly tranquil and beautiful, and Barr a
pleasant Conservation Village.

Refer to Gazetteer for information on: Maybole, Girvan,
Ballantrae, Barr.

TOUR ELEVEN
Ayr to Patna (A712), Dalmellington, Carsphairn, St. John's
Town of Dalry, New Galloway, Newton Stewart (A712),
Challoch (A714), Lochton (B7027), Barrhill, Girvan (A714),
Ayr (A77).

This Tour takes you to lovely Loch Doon.   You travel in the
(legendary) footsteps of John the Baptist.   It also takes you
through the finest part of the great Galloway Forest, with wide
views of hills and lonely fells.   Lochs and mountains dominate the
few roads.

Refer to Gazetteer for information on: Dalmellington, Carsphairn,
St. John's Town of Dalry, New Galloway, Newton Stewart,
Girvan.

TOUR TWELVE

Ayr to Maybole (A77), Crosshill (B7023), Straiton (B741), Stinchar Bridge (Unclassified), Glen Trool, Bargrennan, Barrhill(A714), Pinwherry, Barr (B734), Old Dailly, Dailly (B7023), Wallacetown (unclassified), Maybole (A77), Ayr.

This is certainly one of the finest tours possible. It runs over high and wild country and takes you to Glen Trool. There is no finer view than that from the Bruce Memorial Stone there. Unless, perhaps, it is the one from the top of the near-by Merrick —but you must be equipped for it if you go up there, because that is the highest point in southern Scotland. The country is wild and very beautiful. The contrast between the magnificence of the high moors and mountains, and the gentleness of the land near the coast is very striking. There are some fine walks sign-posted from Stinchar Bridge, and if there has been recent rain, the walk to the Stinchar Falls is especially worth doing.

Refer to Gazetteer for information on: Maybole, Straiton, Glen Trool, Barr.

TOUR THIRTEEN

Ayr to Maidens (A719), Girvan (A77), Ballantrae, Stranraer, Glenluce (A75), Newton Stewart, New Galloway (A712), Carsphairn (A713), Dalmellington, Ayr.

Although a longer tour than some of the others, this is the one for lovers of old buildings and gardens. Both Glen App and Castle Kennedy gardens are included, and there is a long run down the coast, with magnificent views of Arran and Ailsa Craig — and even of the Mull of Kintyre if the day is clear. It is a fine coast, with lots of beaches, rocks and cliffs. There is a visit to the lovely Abbey at Glenluce, and the Tour goes on to cover, again (on the principle that you really can't have too much of a good thing), the wonderful forest road from Newton Stewart to New Galloway.

Refer to Gazetteer for information on: Girvan, Ballantrae, Stranraer, Glenluce, Newton Stewart, New Galloway, Carsphairn, Dalmellington.

TOUR FOURTEEN

Ayr to Maybole (A77), Crosshill (B7023), Balloch (Unclassified), Nick o' the Balloch, Glen Trool, Challoch (A714) Corseriggan (Unclassified), Glenluce, New Luce, Miltonise, Barrhill (A714) Girvan (A77), Ayr.

Apart from the last stretch, this Tour stays away from the coast, and is designed for those who particularly like to be high up on the tops. It is all quite delightful. If you missed Glenluce on Tour Thirteen, with its beautiful and very touching Abbey, there is another chance to see it today, and this time it certainly should not be missed.

Refer to Gazetteer for information on: Maybole, Balloch, Glen Trool, Glenluce, Girvan.

THE MERRICK

GAZETTEER

AILSA CRAIG. This great island rock dominates the Ayrshire coast from Girvan to Stranraer, even though it lies ten miles offshore.

Ailsa can be visited by boat from Girvan, and the trip, at least on a fine day, is memorable. Come to that, it is probably even more memorable on a stormy day! And if you want to be sure of a fine day, then pay attention to the old saw:-

> *When Ailsa Craig pits on its top,*
> *Ye may be sure it's gaun tae to be wat.*
> *When roon about pits on her tie,*
> *Then ye ken, it's gaun tae be dry.*

Ailsa is in fact the vast plug of a long vanished volcano, and its volcanic granite, very close-grained, was long used to make the world's best curling stones. Inevitably, since it lies about half way between Belfast and Glasgow, it is often known as 'Paddy's Milestone'. Indeed, tradition has it that the massive rock, almost 1000 feet high, was once held, around 1000 A.D., by the great Irish King, Brian Boru.

> *Bad luck to the gossoon, spalpeen, or idle Saxon drone,*
> *Who filthy lucre would make out of Brian's precious stone.*

But the curling stone manufacturers seem to have suffered little from the old Irish curse.

Ailsa Craig is, of course, in a very strategic position for controlling the shipping in the Firth of Clyde, and in past years various enterprising mariners used Ailsa as a base for levying toll on passing ships — to the great distress of those on their lawful occasions, and to the considerable anger of those engaged in the very lucrative and common smuggling trade.

In 1597, though, there was a more serious situation, when the Catholic Hew Barclay of Kilbirnie seized and fortified the rock in the interests of Spain. However, a stout Protestant priest, Andrew Knox of Paisley, a relative of John Knox, organised and led a raiding party, which was very successful, and he thrust the Laird of Ladyland off the Craig, and he was *'drownit and perisheit in his awne willfull and desperate resolutions.'*

In more peaceful days, but not so long ago, the multitude of seabirds on Ailsa provided valuable food, which was eaten not only by the few people on the island, but was exported to much of southern Scotland. Today, the birds are of course protected, and there is a great gannetry of five or six thousand birds, whose majestic 6 foot wing span makes their flight most impressive to see. Puffins and guillemots are also there in great numbers, although not perhaps so plentiful as in the days when one tenant farmer, for a wager, killed eighty dozen puffins in one day, knocking them down with a long pole. A few wild Soay sheep and feral goats still live on the Craig. So do three lighthouse keepers, the only people to live permanently on the rock these days.

There are two paths behind the lighthouse, where the boat from Girvan lands its passengers if the sea and weather permit. One leads to an old castle, which was a ruin 400 years ago, but still faces the Atlantic roar. About 800 feet up from the sea is Garry Loch, and close to sea level is M'Nall's Cave, an old smugglers' den, which is about 100 long, 12 feet wide and 20 feet high.

Before the days of radio, and when tenants still lived on the Craig, pigeons were used to summon help, if needed, from Girvan, and coloured flames were shown at night if the lifeboat was required.

The mystery and romance of Ailsa Craig has long impressed poets.   Both Keats and Wordsworth used Ailsa in verses, and in 'Duncan Grey', Burns said that *'Meg was deaf as Ailsa Craig.'* Nothing, indeed, could be more deaf, although Ailsa's voice, of unending surf pounding on unyielding granite, and the plaint of a multitude of sea birds, is far from dumb.

AILSA CRAIG FROM BALLANTRAE

ALLOWAY.   Today, Alloway is hardly separated from Ayr
— it is little more than a pleasant residential suburb.   It must have
been a very different road to travel when Tam o' Shanter made his
midnight ride past a dozen frightening landmarks.   However,
suburb or not, every visitor to Ayrshire, or to any other part of
South-west Scotland, rightly regards a visit to Alloway as being
imperative.   It was there that Robert Burns was born, there that
Tam o' Shanter beheld the dance of witches in the Auld Kirk, and
there is the bridge over which Tam fled, and where his grey mare
Meg lost her tail.   Alloway houses the Burns Monument and the
Burns Centre.   Altogether, the Burns Industry *is* Alloway.   But it
must be seen, for all that.

Most impressive, perhaps, is the *'auld clay biggin'* built by
William Burnes for his new wife and unborn child.   (It was Robert
and his brother Gilbert who changed the family name from
'Burnes' to 'Burns'.)   That little cottage is a simple structure, not
too much changed from that cold January day in 1759 when Robert
was born in the bedplace that is still there.   A few days later *'the
cauld Januar wind blew hansel in on Robin'* as a gable wall
collapsed in a gale, and mother and child had to be moved to a
neighbour's house until repairs were made.   Although not original
to the house or even to the Burnes family, the few simple
furnishings give a clear picture of the simplicity and even starkness
of life in Ayrshire 200 years ago.

Contrasting greatly, and perhaps sadly, with the austerity of the
birthplace is the ornate Memorial built in 1820, to a design by
Thomas Hamilton.   On the triangular base, each side of which
faces one of Ayrshire's districts, is a circular peristyle of nine
Corinthian pillars, which in turn is surmounted by a cupola
crowned by a gilt tripod and supported by three inverted dolphins.
The Memorial contains several relics, including Jean Armour's
wedding ring, and, ironically, Highland Mary's Bible, which was in
effect *her* wedding ring.

Had one tithe of the money spent on that ornate edifice been contributed to the man himself during his poverty and last fatal illness, perhaps he would have lived longer and contributed even more to the pleasures and emotions of humanity.

The Burns Museum is a treasure house of Burns manuscripts and editions from all over the world. Nothing could show more clearly the grip that Burns took on the hearts and minds of people the world over. The greatest of Scotland's literary children, his poems and songs have forged a chain of love surmounting all frontiers and languages, and the manifold editions, in many tongues, show this.

Being in Alloway, of course, it would be unnatural not to walk across the old bridge, and round the old church. Visit the Land o' Burns Centre also, and see the Burns Industry running under a full head of steam. To be fair, though, exhibits in the Land o' Burns Centre do make some effort to show the miserable, grinding poverty endured by the Scottish peasants, and by Burns himself.

The Centre has an excellent craft shop and book shop, and the 'audio-visual display' is of great value as an introduction to Burns's life and work.

AYR. Although on the coast (and a fine, sandy coast it is), Ayr is very much the centre of Ayrshire. Of course, Ayrshire itself has vanished into the vast, amorphous and totally ridiculous Region of Strathclyde. It has been decreed that many another ancient and well-loved name shall also vanish — Dumfriesshire, for example, and the Stewartry of Kirkcudbright. They may have vanished from the files of the bureaucrats, but not from common useage.

The sands of Ayr are a great delight, offering two and half miles of safe bathing, with spectacular views of the Firth of Clyde to Arran. A summer sunset over Arran — and the summer sunsets come late in Ayrshire — is a delight not to be missed. In that magic half hour of the gloaming, the sky is bedecked with a myriad shades of orange and red, and the Sleeping Warrior of Arran is clear in black silhouette. As the glow dims, and Ailsa Craig vanishes into night, the lighthouses take up their task of reminding us that these waters were once a great highway, connecting Scotland with countries many and far.

An ancient town, with a Burgh Charter going back to 1205, Ayr today does not offer the wealth of historical interest one might expect. It is, of course, pre-eminently the town of Robert Burns, and indeed one can tire of the relentless commercial exploitation of Burns. Nevertheless, hidden and shy, as though sheltering from a Council intent on modernisation, there are a number of places well worth looking at in Ayr — quite apart from the 'bonny lasses' noted by Burns!

One of Scotland's oldest houses, Loudoun Hall, still stands in the Boat Vennel, just by the busy New Bridge. Built around 1503 by one James Tait, a wealthy burgess of the town, it is a semi-fortified house, and needed to be in those troubled days, when rival

lairds roistered and battled through the countryside. With three fine vaulted rooms on the ground floor, and a main hall directly above that, the house has small windows built high for defence. The balconies were not designed for taking the air, but rather served as convenient means of waste disposal. In those days, the feared cry of *'Gardy Loo!'*, followed or preceded by an almighty splash, was not confined to Edinburgh. That was the accepted way of disposing of the household slops.

The Boat Vennel itself is old, and was described in St. John's Church Obit. Book of 1533 as *'Ye Vennel passand to ye say.'*

The harbour itself is nearby, and always worth visiting. If you want to see the fish being landed, though, you will have to be up early. The harbour is not so busy in these days as it was in the past, but there is usually a ship or two loading or unloading there,

TAM O' SHANTER INN

A visit to the Land of Burns should include a visit to the Tam O' Shanter Inn. This historic building, the starting point of 'Tam's' immortal ride to Alloway Kirk, is now open to the public as a Museum, containing many interesting exhibits connected with Robert Burns and his epic story of 'Tam O' Shanter'.

Open daily (except Sundays)
April to September   9.30 a.m. to 5.30 p.m.
October to March   12 noon to 4 p.m.
During June, July, August, Sundays 2.30 p.m. to 5 p.m.
Admission: Adults 35p.   School children 20p.

TAM O' SHANTER MUSEUM, AYR.

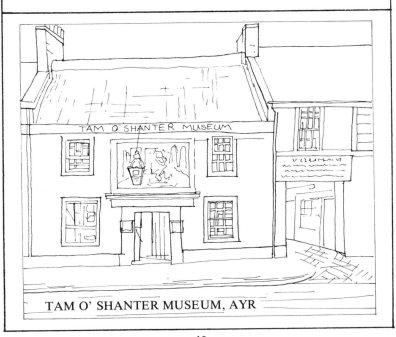

TAM O' SHANTER MUSEUM, AYR

and everyone seems to like watching that, and perhaps dreaming of distant shores.

The prominent Wallace Tower in High St., which conveniently slows both traffic and pedestrians, is of no great age. It was built in 1834 on the site of an older small baronial tower of 1473. A rather feeble statue of William Wallace by the local sculptor Thom is on the side of the tower. It pays but little honour to the great Wallace, whose heroic struggle for his people, and whose ghastly, tormented death at the hands of his English captors, surely demand a more fitting monument. There is a legend that the statue was originally a fine one, but that someone made a bad measurement, and six inches had to be cut out of the legs before it would fit into the niche where it now stands. Sounds like some D.I.Y. jobs of today.

A much better statue is that of Robert Burns, in Burns Statue Square. Although no cold bronze could ever recapture the warmth of that Ayrshire farmer and universal poet, George Lawson's statue strives hard. However, to appreciate it, and to pay the homage which is due, you must be careful to position yourself so that the eye is not distracted by modern ugliness, surely one of the most atrocious pieces of 'Town Planning' in Scotland.

The parish church, which lies behind the Wallace Tower, is interesting in a quiet way, not least for being the church in which Burns was baptised. Two mortsafes (great iron boxes designed to fit over coffins and defeat the ever-vigilant body-snatchers) can be seen in the kirk. There are quite a few of these in Ayrshire (two in Alloway Auld Kirk). It seems that the Burke and Hare body-snatching industry was popular and profitable.

The church was built in 1653, and Cromwell arranged a considerable contribution to its cost. Which was only fair, since his troops demolished the old church in order to build an enormous fort. Hardly a trace of that remains today, except a few inconspicuous bits of wall on the south side of the harbour. Since

Cromwell complained about the cost of building the fort, asking with his puritan voice whether it was being built of gold, it is rather surprising that so little remains.   With luck, some modern examples of architectural meglomania will vanish just as quickly.

However briefly one stays in Ayr, one thing not to be missed is the Auld Brig.   This venerable bridge, which is certainly more than 500 years old, is still an essential pedestrian way, and well maintained.   Burns, of course, wrote of it in *'The Twa Brigs'*. The poem is a conversation, or rather a slanging match, between the proud new bridge and the old one.   The new bridge describes its opponent as a *'Poor narrow footpath of a street, where twa wheelbarrows tremble when they meet.'*   The old bridge replies that *'I'll be a brig when you're a shapeless cairn.'*   And so it was.   The proud new bridge was destroyed by flood and replaced by the present one in 1877, while the old bridge still stands proud.

Also not to be missed in Ayr is the simple and unpretentious Tam o' Shanter museum.   This little building is the original inn from which Tam made his immortal ride on that stormy midnight. Burns must have been familiar with it as an inn, and it would not be strange to him today, could he but return.

Perhaps the best of Ayr is in Wellington Square, and the streets around there.   Well-designed houses, well maintained, still give an inkling of the life and vivacity of the town when these were the town-houses of the wealthy, when the square resounded nightly with music and the rich danced into the dawn.   Then, Ayr was a centre for gaiety and fun — for those rich enough to be admitted to the circle.   Today, the houses are occupied by solicitors and other professional people, a far cry indeed from the *dolce vita* of the mid-19th. century.   The western side of Wellington Square is graced by a fine County Building, and disgraced by an abominable Pavilion, whose exterior is matched only by its interior.   Beyond that, if you can avert your eyes from calamity, is nothing but a vast panorama of sea and sky.

If you like your gardens very colourful and carefully cultivated, then Ayr is the place. Like many another town and indeed village in South-west Scotland, Ayr is a positive rainbow of colour during the summer. Belleisle, Rozelle and Craigie Parks are always well worth seeing. Ayr has repeatedly and regularly won the title of 'Scotland's Floral Town' and 'Britain's Floral Town', and you will understand why.

Near Ayr, on the road south, is the large but quite unobtrusive Butlin's Holiday Camp. For the young in heart and body, a day admission ticket is great value. All the fun of the fair, and much more. Candy Floss and roundabouts and funny hats. Knobbly Knees Competitions vie with Glamorous Granny Contests. Great stuff, and all with a distinct flavour of haggis and tartan!

AYR HIGH STREET

BALLANTRAE. South of Girvan, the road to Ballantrae is delightful, hugging the sea closely, with Ailsa Craig brooding magnificently off-shore. Much of the coast is rock-bound, but there are many tiny beaches, and the rockpools and rocks make for excellent scrambling and beach-combing.

About four miles south of Girvan, the road leaves the coast, which is very rocky at that point, and climbs over Kennedy's Pass, before dropping down again to the coast.

A little further on is Lendal Foot, which is in a magnificent position, but somewhat spoiled by a rash of wooden bung-alows. A few hundred yards inland is the ruin of Carleton Castle, the home of the wicked Sir John Cathcart. As the old ballad describes it, Sir John had the practice of marrying rich girls, then taking them to the top of the cliffs at Games Leap and pushing them off the cliff. Being mean as well as wicked, he made them strip naked first, so that he benefited from the very clothes they were wearing, as well as from their wealth. However, his eighth victim, May Cullean — one of the Kennedys of Culzean—bested him. She asked him to turn away as she stripped, 'for no man should see a naked woman.' He did so, and she pushed *him* over the cliff. The lairds of those days certainly got up to some peculiar tricks.

After leaving Lendal Foot, and before reaching Ballantrae, the road passes over the cliffs of Bennane Head. Be thankful that you live in the present, and not a few hundred years ago, for had you been a traveller on this road then, you may well have fallen victim to the terrible Sawney Bean and his fearful family.

They lived in the caves beneath Bennane Head, and waylaid travellers, killed them, and ate their bodies.

BRIDGE AT BALLANTRAE

45

DOORWAY, BALLANTRAE CHURCH

Originally only Sawney (which is Ayrshire for 'Sandy': Bean is from the Gaelic for 'Fair') and his wife, as time passed the family grew to forty six people, and their escapades were so successful that they had to smoke and cure parts of their victims, presumably against a rainy day.

Sawney was born in the 16th century near Edinburgh, but that area was too well populated for his particular trade. So he moved to the remote area of Ballantrae, which had few people living in it, but a good amount of traffic heading for Ireland and on pilgrimage to Whithorn. The fact that travellers were going missing was noted, of course, and, as a contemporary account put it, *'abundance of innocent travellers and innkeepers were executed on suspicion of being murderers, yet all was in vain.*

It was James VI — he who hated tobacco and was not too keen on women — who finally hunted down Sawney, with the help of 400 men and a large number of dogs. The forty six Beans, who it was estimated had killed over 1000 people, were executed barbarously, the women on the spot and the men publicly in Edinburgh, for the delectation of the crowd.

The awful doings in the Bennane Head Caves were useful for the smugglers of a later age. Few people indeed would venture near the place, and the smugglers made full use of them.

With a little luck, incidentally, you might, if it is the right time of year, see fulmars nesting on the cliffs above the road at Bennane Head.

Ballantrac Bay was the very heart of the smuggling trade. In his **'History of the County of Ayr'** Paterson records that:-

> *'Large vessels called buckers, lugger rigged, carrying 20 or 30 guns, were in the habit of landing their cargoes in the bay of Ballantrae, while a hundred lintowers, some armed with cutlasses and pistols, might be seen waiting with their horses to receive them, to convey the goods by unfrequented paths through the country and even to Edinburgh and Glasgow. Many secret holes, receptacles for contraband articles, still exist, in the formation of which much skill and cunning is shown. The old Kirk....contained one of the best......*(for) *it appears that the ruling elder was the chief and centre of a very extensive smuggling body on this coast.'*

Ballantrae is graced by the ruins of Ardstinchar Castle, once the home of the Kennedys of Bargany. The two main branches of the Kennedy family, those of Cassilis and those of Bargany, fought long and hard for the overlordship of Carrick. Neither gained clear victory, and the only sure losers were the serfs and the families of the serfs who fought and died and were plundered in strife which could never benefit them. Sir Walter Scott, whose romantic view of Scottish history still distorts reality, wrote of those Kennedy struggles in *'Auchendraine'*, and so did the local writer S.R. Crockett in *'The Grey Man'*.

Hard by Ardstinchar Castle is the beautiful Stinchar Bridge, carrying the road over the mouth of the river Stinchar. Often, when the river is low, many salmon can be seen in the pools by the bridge, waiting for sufficient water to get up river to their spawning grounds beyond Stinchar Bridge. They have a perilous journey: not only must they face the hazards of many fishermen, but also of many wild mink, which kill salmon, eat a little from the throat, and leave the rest to rot.

Stevenson, incidentally, did not place his novel *'Master of Ballantrae'* in Ballantrae, but merely borrowed the name, and placed the action in Borgue, Galloway. Perhaps he did that out of pique, for legend has it that he was once stoned by the inhabitants of Ballantrae, and chased out of the village because of the outlandish clothes he wore!

BALLOCH. If you travel south from Ayr on the A 77, after six miles you pass through the little village of Minishant. Just half a mile further on, a minor road on the left will lead you (follow the signposts) to Crosshill.

Continue straight through the village to the hamlet of Cloyntie, and there cross straight over the main road on to the mountain road to Newton Stewart. This, an unclassified road, runs through some of the wildest and most beautiful country in all of South-west Scotland, even if many of the hillsides are now covered in the monotonous conifers of the Forestry Commission. Twisting round the De'ils Elbow, the road runs past the Pilot Hill and Craigenmaddie, with Garleffin Fell on the other side. This is rare and wild country; country which in the long summer gloaming can be gentle and welcoming, but on a day of snow or driving rain can be savage and unforgiving. It is in the real sense a high road, reaching 1107 feet before dropping down to the richness of the Stinchar valley.

Just before you reach the valley, there are some very prominent old turf dykes, prehistoric defenses, on the right, up the flank of Daljedburgh Hill. See them soon, before afforestation hides them for ever.

At Balloch, continue straight across the road junction, and begin the steep climb through conifer plantations to Nick o' the Balloch. After a mile or so of plantations, you very suddenly find yourself on an open hillside with a precipitous fall on the right and an equally steep slope on the left. The road clings to the hillside, still climbing steeply, and the valley floor drops further and further below. The road is actually climbing dramatically up the shoulder of Eldrick Hill, with the steep and cruel scree slopes of Craigenreoch across the valley.

49

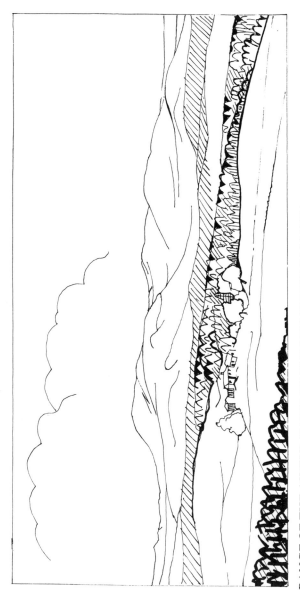

RANGE OF THE AWFUL HAND, FROM NICK OF THE BALLOCH

A 'Nick' is a pass or saddle, and 'Balloch' is a corruption of the Gaelic *'Bealach'* or 'Pass', and at the Nick o' the Balloch, you will have climbed to 1118 feet.   Stop at a convenient place at the very top, and take a long look at the Range of the Awful Hand before you.

There, and stretching far to the south-east, lie the vast and rounded mountains of Ayrshire and Galloway.   Tarfessock (2228 ft.), Kirriereoch (2565 ft.), Merrick (2764 ft.), Benyallery (2360 ft.), are the fingers of the Awful Hand, and, further south, Bennon is the thumb.   North of the range is Shalloch-on-Minnoch (2520 ft.), Shalloch (1777 ft.), and Cairnmadloch (1558 ft.)   All the names, and the name of the range itself, are from the Gaelic, and remind us that not so long ago Gaelic was the language of this corner of Scotland.

Looking at these hills, you will well understand the local writer, S.R. Crockett, who wrote that this range is a *'weird, wild world, new and strange, not yet out of chaos — not yet approved of God.'*

Whenever you stand at the Nick o' the Balloch and look over that Range, the emptiness and majesty of it will impress very deeply.   The colours, the shapes, the shadows, the great emptiness, and, over all the vastness of the sky, combine to make a harmony difficult to match.   To see it on a summer evening, soft in its gentleness and coloured shadows, is an experience.   To see it on a wild autumn day, with the rain showers chasing each other over the great whale-backs of the hills, is another experience altogether.   But the finest experience of all, perhaps, is to see it on a winter day after a snowfall, and when the sky is blue again. Then, the Range of the Awful Hand is truly majestic.

Just by the Nick is an old well.   This is the Brandy Well, and tradition has it that the smugglers passing through from the coast to the cities let their horses drink there, and that a small keg of brandy was sometimes added to the water, for the horses, if the pace was swift.

Until the new road was cut (and it is still narrow enough, and single-tracked), the climb up the Nick was very steep and dangerous. Traces of the old track can still be seen on the left as you climb to the summit.

Continue from the Nick across open moorland to the first road junction, and turn left on the unclassified road leading to Straiton. Tradition has it that an inn once stood at that road junction, and that many travellers who stayed there disappeared: they were murdered for their money by the inn-keeper and her family.

The road continues over wild and open moorland, with Eldrick Hill (1593 ft.) on the left and Shalloch on the right. Within a mile or two is the summit, with a board showing the height as 1421 ft.

After dropping down a short way, Stinchar Bridge is reached. This is an ideal centre for walking and fishing. On Forestry Commission land, it represents the more acceptable face of the Commission. There is car parking, a few simple benches and tables and instructions for a whole series of walks over the hills. The walks are not particularly strenuous or long, but all are worth while. And even at the height of summer you are unlikely to meet more than a small handful of people. You can indeed choose your own hillside, and have it to yourself for all of an idyllic summer afternoon.

If you feel adventurous, a rough county road runs off to the east (your right) just past Stinchar Bridge. This will lead you, by a great rocky wilderness, over the moors to Loch Bradan. Actually, this is two lochs, now joined since the outlet was dammed to provide a water supply to Ayr. Raising the level of the water drowned an ancient castle that stood on the shores of Loch Bradan. It is a lonely road, and you have to return the way you went, but for the car traveller it perhaps takes you further into the midst of the hills than you can reach any other way. Very much worth while.

FULMAR

OLD MORTALITY, BALMACLLELAN

BALMACLELLAN. A small, delightful, steep village, just east of New Galloway on the Dumfries road. A lovely and quiet place, it was the home of Robert Paterson, the original of Scott's 'Old Mortality'. He wandered the whole of Lowland Scotland, seeking out the graves of Covenanters, cleaning them, and if necessary carving crude stones to mark them.

There is a statue of Old Mortality and his equally old horse at Holm House, Balmaclellan. Perhaps it is not a particularly fine statue, and it was done by an amateur sculptor, but it is remarkably touching. He is there just as Scott described him — his bonnet, stout shoes and cloth leggings. His horse, head drooping, stands by, saddled with a sack of straw. Old Mortality has his chisel in his hand, resting on a stone slab, as though he had just been interrupted in his self-imposed task.

And having admired the statues, please then complain as loudly as you can to anyone who will listen that these delightful mementoes of Scotland's past are almost buried by rubbish, and apparently forgotten.

BARR. This attractive Ayrshire village is perhaps best approached from the main Newton Stewart—Girvan road (A 714). About a mile north of Pinwherry on that road, a minor road on the right (B 734), signposted Barr, leads to the village. Incidentally, two tiny settlements on the same lane near Pinwherry are called Muckfoot and Bellymore!

Immediately after leaving the main Girvan road and crossing the river, there is a short and steep hill, with a very sharp bend. This should be treated with care, for there is little warning of it. You now travel for a few miles along the valley of the Stinchar, and there is perhaps no more pleasant valley in all of Ayrshire.

Robert Burns, of course, knew the valley well. Indeed, there are persistent legends that he did some courting, and left traces of it, in more than one of the farms along the valley floor.

He wrote:

> *Beyond yon hill where Stinchar flows,*
> *Mang muirs and mosses many, O,*
> *The weary sun the day has clos'd,*
> *An' I'll awa' tae Nannie, O.*

Unfortunately, he was persuaded to change 'Stinchar' to 'Lugar'. Even in those days, it seems that there were people who supposed that the '*ch*' in Stinchar should be pronounced as a '*k*' sound, instead of a soft '*sh*'. Such people exist to this day, and some should know better. Burns listened perhaps too intently to those who sought to explain 'good taste' to him. Consequently, we have been deprived of some good work. Even *Tam o' Shanter* suffered from the 'unco guid', who advised Burns to delete, from the list of ghastly objects displayed on the Holy Table, a vivid and uncomplimentary description of lawyers' tongues, priests' hearts and well-sealed doctors' bottles!

About two miles after turning right onto the B 734, there is the very fine Cairn o' Cairnwhin on the north side of the road — your

left.   It is easily seen as it stands on a hillock.   Nothing seems to be known about it, nor has it ever been excavated.

About two miles before reaching Barr, you will pass, on the north bank of the river (your left), the site of a very famous and long lasting fair.   This was held around the old church of Kirkdominae, or perhaps Kirkdamdie, or even Kirkdandy.   This was at a farm still called Kirkland.   The church itself is something of a mystery, for there is no record of when it was built, nor by whom.   Certainly it was built before 1300, and in 1404 King Robert III assigned the 'Chapel of the Holy Trinity of Koldomine' to Crossraguel Abbey. Many of the stones of the old church were used to build a new church at Barr, but even that new church has now gone, to be replaced by one even newer.

Quietness and serenity today mark the site of the old chapel, of which the only trace is an arch above a Holy Well.   It seems, and it is strange, that during its long history the old church did not attract even the smallest village.

And yet, in spite of its lonely position, Kirkdominae Fair was a great occasion.   It was originally a Hiring Fair, but must also have been a wonderful day out, on a Saturday in May, for families from miles around.   It was held until 1860, and towards the end there were more than fifty tents selling whisky!

> *Some did the thieving trade pursue,*
> *While ithers cam' to sell their 'oo,*
> *An' ithers cam' tae weet their mou,*
> *An' gang wi' lasses hame, mon.*

And surely many of the lasses did not reach home by the most direct route!

A contemporary writer, just before the last days of the fair, said that the fair *'Long had a celebrity in the Western Shires quite equal to that of Donnybrook in the Sister Isle.'*   And we have all heard of the shennanigans at Donnybrook!

Barr village — and it is always, and always has been, called 'The Barr' by local people — is entered by a narrow arched bridge over the Water of Gregg Burn, which joins the Stinchar a hundred yards away.

The Barr is a Conservation Village, and much of it pretty. Although dominated by the great mass of Auchensoul Hill across the river (*Barr* means: a ridge or high hill), the village is a fine sun-trap of a place. Bowling and putting are available, fishing, of course, and a most excellent home-made tea is served in the village hall. The church, which is directly across the Gregg Bridge, was built in 1878 (at a price of £892 :15 :0). It is always open, and always welcoming.

In 1837, the Rev. Ebenezer Wallace recorded that Barr then contained 230 people, mostly weavers and traders, and that this was an increase over earlier years. He noted that the population outside the village was declining, due to amalgamation of farms, which thus required fewer workers. The people on the whole, he said, were healthy, but palsy (!) was prevalent. One wonders why. Could it be connected with the fact that Barr was also on a direct smugglers' route to the north? Perhaps there was an early equivalent of goods 'falling off the back of a lorry'!

There is a delightful myth about the Laird of Changue, who lived in Barr in the Good Old Days. The Laird was quite a character, well known and feared for his roistering and fighting. Wishing to acquire even more wealth, he made a pact with the Devil himself that he would give up his immortal soul to Auld Hornie in return for great wealth. The Devil, as he always did in those days, kept his word, and the Laird prospered. However, when the time came to deliver up his soul, the Laird refused to keep his side of the bargain. The two fought a great battle on the hill above Changue House, and the Devil, minus tail, horns and wings, retired beaten, leaving the Laird to enjoy his wealth and die happy. The myth does not tell us where his soul went then. The story must be true,

BARR

for Changue House still stands, and any inhabitant of Barr will be happy to point out the Devil's Footprints, where no grass grows, on the hill above the house.

There is an interesting Covenanter's gravestone in the churchyard.   The stone reads:

1685
HEAR LYES EDW
ARD McKEEN W
HO WAS ShoAT IN
THIS PARISh BY C
ORN DOUGLLAS F
Or ADherANCE TO
THE WOrD OF GOD
AND SCOTLLANDS
COUeNATeD WOrK
OF REFORmATION.

On the other side of the stone there is a sand-glass and below it a hand holding a tablet bearing the words:

BE FAITH
FUL UNT
O DEAT
H &c.

Edward McKeen was not an inhabitant of Barr, but was visiting to buy corn.   Prayers were being held in a private house when the soldiers arrived, and while the others escaped, Edward hid between two cottages, having no house to run to.   He was discovered, and shot out of hand.

As you leave the village on the Girvan road, crossing the Stinchar by another delightful arched bridge, straight in front is a tiny cottage, lodge house to Alton Albany.   The cottage nestles comfortably amongst huge old trees, and is so much at home it seems to have grown there.

On the Girvan road (B734), you climb steeply above the Stinchar valley.   This road is known locally as The Screws, and you will understand why. The views down the valley and across the hills are quite spectacular. Just past the first road junction you pass the gates of Penkill Castle. D.G. Rossetti spent long vacations and wrote much there in the 1860's. While resting in a cave above the castle — or sleeping — he was visited by a raven which warned him against violating his wife's grave (he had been thinking of doing so) to recover some poems he had buried with her. Other pre-Raphaelites, including William Morris, often visited Penkill. Indeed, one of them, William Bell Scott, died there. The Castle still contains much of their work and is a repository of some of the finest, indeed, unique, examples of Pre-Raphaelite artistry. The castle can be visited, but only by prior arrangement, and in small parties. The little effort involved is very much worth while, though, particularly if you are shown round by the present owner, a very knowledgeable and articulate American, who has done much to restore and preserve the castle and its irreplaceable contents.

Just past the Castle gates, continue down the hill to the road junction. Immediately in front is a very romantic-looking and well-preserved ruined church. It is well worth a visit for its sheer simplicity and homeliness. The church was deserted 250 years ago, when a new one was built in New Dailly nearby. The old one has a tiny bell-cote at each end, and contains a Kennedy mausoleum. In the churchyard are the Charter Stones. These are two rounded boulders, obviously glacier-borne from afar, and, in the old days, it was a test of strength and manhood to lift them. Indeed, it probably would be still.

There was a ford over the Water of Girvan by the church, leading to the Baron's Stone of Killochan. This great boulder was also glacier-borne from the shore of Loch Doon, and it marked a place of assembly and justice. Rough, doubtless.

Eastward, Hadyard Hill still bears great Pictish earthworks, clearly visible at the west end of the ridge. Very recently,

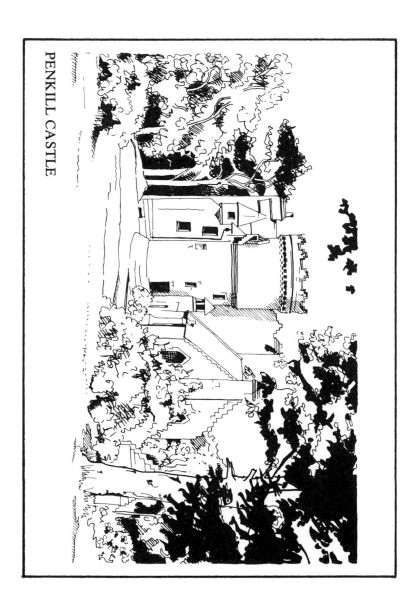

PENKILL CASTLE

63

excavations by a group of local young people, led by a local police officer, have uncovered a tiny chapel on Barony Hill. It is possible that this is the earliest Christian site in Ayrshire, and may be a chapel built by St. Machar, who came to Scotland with St. Columba, and proseletysed extensively, as far away as Aberdeen, where the present-day Cathedral is named after him. St. Machar's Chapel was known 200 years ago, but was then lost again.

Turn right at the road junction opposite the ruined church, on to the Crosshill — Straiton road, which is unclassified. After a mile or so, on the left, is Bargany House. The grounds are very much worth visiting. There is a wonderful variety of trees and shrubs, all in a most natural setting, with ponds and streams and flowers in rock outcrops. During a previous economic recession, unemployed weavers from Girvan built a lovely walk in the gardens, still known as The Weavers' Walk. There is also a very fine bridge over the Water of Girvan, which flows through the grounds.

Altogether, a wholly delightful place. No charge is made for admission nor for car parking, and anyone who does not contribute generously into the box by the car park fully deserves a visit by a ghoulie.

From Bargany, the road, now B 7023, passes the outskirts of Dailly, or New Dailly, and runs through pleasant country with the great roll of Hadyard Hill to the right. The church at Dailly is interesting, and worth the short diversion. It has a curious steeple, and three lairds' lofts, for the local landowners of Bargany, Dalquharran and Kilkerran.

The two castles of Dalquharran are clearly visible from the road. The younger of the two was designed by Robert Adam in 1786, just as Culzean was. It is a massive building, and really no less beautiful than Culzean. Now, though, the roof has been removed, and the lovely building left to the owls, the bats and the vandals. The old castle, just to the south, is a 16th century ruin, and very romantic. There are the remains of a walled garden, the family graveyard, and some interesting tombs.

<hr>

BEESWING.　There is really nothing much to say about Beeswing, although it is certainly a pleasant enough Galloway village.　But what a name!　More particularly since the next village is Lotus!

The name 'Beeswing' actually derives from a famous racehorse of a century and a half ago.　She was a two year old in her first race, and in eight seasons entered 64 major races and won 51 of them.　When her owner, Robert Orde, retired, he bought the Inn at the village then called Lochend, and renamed the Inn 'The Beeswing'.　Over the years, that name gradually attached itself to the village, and today even the maps give it that name, although the Church is still known as Lochend Church.

If you want to visit Beeswing and Lotus, travel on the A 711 between Dumfries and Dalbeatie.

South-west Scotland has many rare place-names.　Perhaps the strangest group is in north Ayrshire, where Moscow lies on the Volga river near Irvine.　The village has both Higher and Lower Rushaw Farms, and Random Rouble House is close by!　Also in Ayrshire is the village of Maidens, well worth visiting if for no other reason than that you will be able to boast, quite honestly, that you have visited Scottish Maidens on your holiday!

In his remarkable and neglected book *'Land of the Leal',* James Barke includes a long list of place-names from the Stranraer district.　It is a wonderful list, ringing like a peal of bells, and worthy of being intoned like some great litany.

BROWN CARRICK HILL.   If you are in the northern part of South-west Scotland, around Ayr, then a visit to Brown Carrick Hill is very much worth while.   If you leave Ayr by the main coast road south (A719), go on by The Heads of Ayr to a minor single track road on the left, leading steeply up a hill.   This is Brown Carrick Hill, and the road is steep and perhaps rather dangerous.   But the result is worthwhile for the view from the top.   Climbing over 900 feet in a mile or so, the narrow road takes you from the rich coastal plain, with its lush dairy land and early potato fields, to a rough highland moor, uncultivated and supporting only a few sheep.   But the thin grass can be gay with tormentil and eyebright, and, if you wander away from the road, you can be rewarded with a dish of blaeberries.   And nothing in the world tastes as good as fresh-picked Ayrshire blaeberries.   Unless, perhaps, it is blaeberry pie.

Blaeberries or not, it is really the view you came for, and that is spectacular indeed.   It must have been a view like this with which Satan tempted Jesus.   The whole Firth of Clyde is below you, with the Highland mountains blue in the distance.   Westward is Arran, and on a fine day, so clear is the air, you feel you could almost shake hands with a walker on Goat Fell over there.   South-ward is the great sweep of the Ayshire coast, with all its rocks and beaches, and Ailsa Craig dreaming away.   Eastward are the great hills and fells of Ayrshire and Galloway.

A view most definitely not to be missed, and one to linger over.   What's more, you may well have it all to yourself, even on a summer day.

CARSPHAIRN. Carsphairn is a quiet moorland village on the main road (A 713) north from New Galloway to Dalmellington and Ayr. Really, it is nothing more than a broad main street, with simple, well-proportioned houses. Like many another such village in Ayrshire and Galloway, there is little of very great interest, yet they are all attractive, couthy places, where the visitor is welcome, and made to feel welcome.

Which ever way you travel it, the A 713 is a fine moorland road, soaring and climbing and ever-changing. At Mossdale, two miles out of Dalmellington to the south, a minor road on the right leads to Loch Doon, and that is very well worth a detour, especially for the most excellent views of the Rhinns of Kells, with Corserine (2669 feet) on the eastern shore of the loch.

The Rhinns are, in order, Black Craig (1730 feet), Corran o' Portmark (2042 feet), Bow, Meaul (2383 feet), and Corserine — which means The Crossings — (2668 feet).

Loch Doon is about six miles long and perhaps half a mile wide. Although it has been considerably enlarged and deepened by the building of two dams, one on the north and one at the south, the Loch is by no means spoiled, and remains one of the loveliest and quietest spots in all of Scotland.

When the dams were built and the water level raised, the island on which Castle Doon stood was totally submerged. The castle itself, though, was moved stone by stone to a new site on the west bank, and today it looks as though it has always been there. It was the castle of the Balliol family, a family of great importance to the history of Scotland.

The road to the Loch runs by the rugged Glen of the Waterfalls. Once, the outflow from the Loch roared and plunged down this glen on its way north to Ayr. Now, more quietly, the water is diverted south, and provides hydro-electricity near Kirkcudbright. The road actually crosses the great dam which impounds the waters.

LOCH DOON

Although the road round the Loch is hardly of motorway quality, it is well worth going as far as the road goes — or as far as your car will safely take you. There is a turning place for vehicles just where the Carrick Lane plunges down, carrying water from Loch Riecawr and Loch Macaterick. (A *'lane'* is a water-course joining two lochs.) Although really only on the edge of the Carrick hills, you can get a sense of their unique beauty from there. And if you care to walk beyond the road, there is even greater peace and solitude.

Loch Doon is fed by remote Loch Enoch, no less than 1617 feet above sea level, and the two are joined by the tempestuous Gala Lane. The banks of the Gala Lane provide a good track into the remote high lands. Of course, walking in the Carrick Hills is not to be compared with a stroll on Sunday afternoon in the park, and you should be properly shod. Just the same, in the hills, walking is the way to go.

CASTLE DOUGLAS. There is no more pleasant town in South-west Scotland — perhaps in all of Scotland — than Castle Douglas. Today basically a market town for the rich surrounding farmlands, it is a fine example of 18th. century town planning, in an age when beauty and order seemed just as important as utility. It is very well served by an excellent road network, enabling the tourist to reach every part of the area, and, very important, allowing you to return without travelling over the same road.

One of the great attractions, of course, is Carlingwark Loch. Not many towns can boast of having a 100 acre loch, tree-lined and island-studded, only a few hundred yards from the town centre. For many centuries, and until quite recently, the Loch seems to have served as a rubbish dump for all the peoples and settlements on its banks, and many items of great beauty have been recovered from it, from the Bronze Age to more recent centuries. Most of these were recovered in the process of dredging up the bottom mud to be spread as fertile marl on the surrounding farms. There is no dredging done these days, and the pike and perch, the yellow waterlilies and the water fowl are left undisturbed.

There are two *crannogs* in the Loch, artificial islands of great logs driven into the bottom and covered with brushwood. These are the forts of Bronze Age people, to be approached only by one easily-defended ford through the water.

Castle Douglas is a great centre for walking. Not the sort of walking that takes you into the lonely hills, but gentle walking over quiet roads and paths. Of all the walks around Castle Douglas, though, perhaps the finest is to the top of Kelton Hill, south-east of the town, past the Loch. From the top of Kelton Hill there are memorable views of loch, mountains and rivers. You can trace the course of the Dee as it winds its way amongst the trees and fields on its way to the Solway. To the south-east is the lovely green swell of Dungyle Hill, crowned by a Roman fort. To the north are the mountain solitudes and grandeurs of Galloway, the

Kells range and the Cairnsmuirs. In the foreground, Threave Castle lies encircled by the Dee.

Of course, it is difficult to think of Castle Douglas and not think of Threave Castle, that magnificent, medieval stronghold of the Black Douglasses, built on its grassy island between two arms of the Dee.

Its origins are really lost and remote in history, but probably it was built by Archibald the Grim. Certainly he died there on Christmas Eve, 1440. He was called 'The Grim', incidentally, by the English, because of his expression when in battle. And the English knew him well in battle!

Originally over 70 feet high, the Castle walls are 8 feet thick, and the whole structure was big enough to allow the Earls of Douglas to quarter one thousand men inside. It was big and strong, and threatened the whole countryside.

However, it did not intimidate Mons Meg. Meg was a great cannon forged by Brawny Kim, the local blacksmith, and his seven sons. That was during the great rebellion of 1453, and Threave was the last castle to hold out for the Black Douglasses. The King, James II, was determined to lead the battle himself. He marched his army into Galloway, and camped by the Three Thorns of Carlingwark, where the town of Castle Douglas now stands. The people of the countryside, long weary of the grinding despotism of the Douglas family, welcomed the King, and each household willingly contributed a bar of iron for the forging of Mons Meg.

Brawny Kim and his sons laboured well, and they produced a cannon (which you can see to this day in the bowels of Edinburgh Castle) thirteen feet long and with a bore of twenty inches. They called it 'Meg', after Kim's wife, also the possessor of a powerful voice.

Meg was loaded with a peck of gunpowder and a granite ball the weight of a Carsphairn cow, so it was said.

Unaware of all this, the defenders of the Castle awaited with no anxiety the usual attack by men and horses. The Douglas himself was not in the Castle, but his wife was. 'The Fair Maid of Galloway', as she was known, was dining when Meg first spoke. The great granite ball shot straight through the Castle and took off the hand of the Fair Maid as she raised a wine cup to her lips. The Castle did not long withstand the battering of Meg, and the King won the day, and kept his Crown. History does not record whether Meg ever spoke again.

There would have been not much regret throughout Galloway at the defeat of the Black Douglasses. They were an exceptionally cruel and ruthless bunch, even in that cruel and ruthless age. In 1452, William, the 8th Earl, boasted that the Gallows Knob at Threave (the stone knob above the gateway, which was used for hangings) 'had not been without a tassle for fifty years.' It was said that to maintain that record, William would casually execute any passing serf if no miscreant was waiting.

Near Castle Douglas, just off to the right from the main A75 road to Dumfries, is the great Mote of Urr, the largest of Scotland's Mote-hills. The origin and purpose of this great artificial hill remains uncertain. What is certain is that it is a most impressive work of early man. A great ditch 8 feet deep and 47 feet wide surrounds an enormous oval hill five hundred long. It rises in three steps to a height of 85 feet, and the flat top is 90 feet by 75 feet. Whatever it was, and whatever might be buried under it, it is well worth a visit, if only to wonder at the stupendous effort required to build such a hill in those days.

ARBIGLAND GARDENS

KIRKBEAN   DUMFRIES

BIRTHPLACE OF JOHN PAUL JONES

SITUATED 2 MILES SOUTH OF KIRKBEAN ON THE A 710

SOLWAY COAST ROAD

Open Tuesday, Thursday, Sunday

May to September   2 - 6 p.m.

TEA ROOM

COLVEND COAST. The Colvend Coast is that triangle of land dipping down into the Solway between Dumfries and Dalbeattie. It is a lovely, quiet area, rich in everything that makes for delight when on holiday.

Dominated by the high hill of Criffell, there are fine beaches along this coast, and excellent sailing on the sheltered waters. Not so very long ago, those same waters were used extensively in the vast smuggling trade which flourished hereabout. Brandy, wine, tobacco and silk — all without the benefit of excise duty — were landed on this coast throughout the 18th century. Robert Burns himself was an excise agent hereabout, based in Dumfries, and he once led an armed attack on a French smuggler beached and waiting for a fresh tide.

New Abbey (with the lovely ruins of Sweetheart Abbey), Kirkbean, Rockcliff and Kippford are the villages on this coast, and all are attractive places. If you walk over the hill between Rockcliff and Kippford, you pass the Mote of Mark, a highly impressive Roman hill-fort, with a splendid view over the coast and over Rough Island, now a bird sanctuary.

CREETOWN. This is a granite town. Built of granite, it is founded upon granite, for in years past the quarries here sent granite to build, amongst many other things, the Thames Embankment and the Mersey Docks. There is little granite quarried these days, though, and the ships no longer come.

Being a granite town, there is a remarkable contrast between Creetown and those other Solway towns built of warm red sandstone. The granite is grey and cool, and the flakes of mica sparkle brightly in the sun. The granite is hard, of course, and does not lend itself to easy carving and decoration, so that the town seems simple and austere, like Aberdeen on a small and homely scale.

The main road, the A75, now runs round the Solway coast to Gatehouse of Fleet, but there is an older military road, unclassified, over the high moors, and it is delightful. It takes you past Rusko Castle and other out-of-the-way places.

Not that the main road should be ignored. Indeed, there is a story that Queen Victoria once asked Thomas Carlyle (who was born not very far away) which was the finest road in her realm. He replied that it was the coast road from Creetown to Gatehouse of Fleet. 'Is there not one as good?' she queried. 'Yes,' he replied, 'The coast road from Gatehouse of Fleet to Creetown!' It was said that in his excitement, Carlyle had edged his chair so close to the Queen that the leg had trapped her skirts, and that there was some difficulty in disentangling them with due decorum.

One thing about Creetown is unique, and that is the Rock and Gem Museum. This is a private collection of rocks, minerals and gems from all over the world, and is one of the largest such in Britain. A visit there will pass a very interesting hour.

Creetown is the centre of the country Scott wrote about in *'Guy Mannering'* and Creetown itself is 'Port-an-Ferry'. Two local castles, Carsluith and Barholm, both claim to be 'Ellengowan'.

Carsluith, 3 miles from Creetown going east, is a fine old airy ruin. Nothing much seems ever to have happened there, except perhaps that it was the birthplace of Gilbert Brown, the last Abbot of Sweetheart Abbey.

Three miles further on, up a hill on the left of the road, is Barholm. John Knox once hid there, and apart from that nothing much seems to have happened there, either. It is a great pity that many of the other Lowland castles did not have such a peaceful existence. The most unusual feature of Barholm is the two stair windows, with each lintel formed from one piece of stone, one of them double-arched and the other an ogee.

Just up Kirkdale Burn from Barholm is Cairn Holy, where Meg Merrilees and her gypsies camped. There are great chambered cairns there, said to be the burial place of the warrior-king Goldeus of Scotland. These are very impressive and very much worth a visit.

Near the mouth of the burn, on the shore below Barholm, is Dirk Hatterick's Cave. It is 30 feet above the beach, and there is a narrow squeeze at the entrance before a steep drop to the floor. It is lined with shelves and pigeon-holes to store smuggled brandy. Or so the story goes, and there is no pleasure in spoiling good stories.

South of Barholm is Ravenshall Point, with truly magnificent rock formations running down to the beach. Watch there for the ravens which give the point its name.

78

CULZEAN CASTLE.

CULZEAN CASTLE. Culzean Castle lies on the road south from Ayr. Wherever you might be staying in South-west Scotland, Culzean is quite simply a 'must' to visit.

There is so much that could be said about the Castle and its grounds that it is perhaps best to say little, except to be as persuasive as possible that you should go and visit it yourself. If the day is fine, wander round the several hundred acres of garden and woodland: if wet, absorb the beauty of the Castle itself. You pay to enter, but the admirable National Trust for Scotland benefits. Indeed, better to join the Trust and visit other sites.

From the 12th century, Culzean was but one of several small Kennedy castles, built chiefly for defensive purposes. In 1775, David, the 10th Earl, called in Robert Adam to rebuild. For the rich and the intellectual that was of course a stirring time, with new ideas, methods, products and ideals coming thick and fast. For Scotland, it was a time of peace and soaring ambition, even if, for the Highlands, it was the peace of death.

Robert Adam, an architect of genius, combined with the wealth of the great Kennedy estate, and with other civilised minds, produced a vast and beautiful romantic concept in a classical age. It is a great castle on a cliff, looking over the water to Arran and beyond, surrounded by 560 acres of woodland and policies. Even the farm buildings were re-designed and built in harmony with the Castle itself.

Yet, for all its beauty, the great and stately pile is somehow out of place in that exposed position. One feels that it should be far inland, sheltered in some green and pleasant valley, instead of facing the Atlantic blasts on that rock-bound shore.

Both the Castle and the grounds are of course maintained immaculately. One feels that the Kennedy's must have just left each room a moment ago. How, though, did they ever fit into that peculiar shoe-shaped bath?

CULZEAN CASTLE

During the Second World War, many Allied commanders and dignitaries stayed at Culzean, and General Eisenhower amongst them.   Later, he was gifted an apartment in the castle for his own use, and stayed there frequently, even when he was President of the United States.   Culzean, of course, is near to some of the finest golf courses in Scotland, and that was a considerable attraction for the President.   His apartment is still preserved as it was in his day, and can be rented by those rich enough to afford it.   An exhibition in the Castle gives a very graphic picture of the days when that part of the Allied forces commanded by Eisenhower was preparing for the landing in France and the eventual link-up with the Russian Allies sweeping in from the east.

The cliffs under the Castle are riddled with caves, and they are great fun to explore.   It is said that in days long past, the Kennedy's took shelter in those caves when their enemies hunted them.   The Park Rangers organise lots of walks and activities in the grounds, and if your interest is in birds or plants you can learn much from them.

You might even hear the Phantom Piper if you visit Piper's Brae, although he has not appeared recently.   He is said to have been a Kennedy piper, murdered by another Kennedy in some obscure conflict in the early 17th century, and still seeking revenge.

The name, incidentally, is pronounced *'Cullane'*.

DALMELLINGTON. Dalmellington is a run-down coal mining and iron-working town, one of the places made by the Industrial Revolution, and now in the process of destruction by the Revolution of Industrial Decline. But, because it was early on the industrial scene, there is much there to interest those who care about our recent past. It is perhaps sad, and it is certainly chastening, to see tools and artifacts of once flourishing industries preserved as curiosities. But they are there in Dalmellington, and they make a visit to the town very worthwhile.

The traditional industries of Dalmellington may have been allowed to die, but the community itself refuses to die. A great effort is being made to stay alive, partly by encouraging tourism.

It will never be a pretty place, but mining and iron working villages never were pretty, anyway, and it would be misleading those who visit here to pretend that it ever was pretty. The Cathcartson Interpretation Centre, in the middle of the town, is a row of skilfully restored old cottages. Inside, the history of Dalmellington is displayed, and it is fascinating. The Ayrshire Valleys Tourist Board certainly has an uphill task, but they try hard.

Fortunately, in a way, Robert Burns had no real connection with Dalmellington, so, for once in South-west Scotland we are not diverted by his towering presence from appreciating other things. At the Interpretation Centre there is a mass of well-displayed information on mining, iron working, Covenanters, agriculture and local history. Photographs, illustrations, text, all combine to give the visitor a quick appreciation of what has been in the not-so-distant past. Surely well worth visiting.

There is also a Rail Preservation Group active in the town, and they have locomotives in steam each Sunday. That is a grand opportunity for the small boy lurking in every one of us.

DUMFRIES. Even if it did not have such close associations with Robert Burns, Dumfries is a town well worth visiting.
Perhaps it is the warm red sandstone used so freely there for
building, but whatever the reason, the town always seems to glow
— a sharp contrast to the cool granite towns further west along the
Solway coast.   And the effect of a welcoming warmth is added to
by the massed flowers which grace the town centre all summer
long, and far into the autumn.

To deal first with Robert Burns, it must be said at once that
Dumfries avoids the more extreme commercial exploitation of him
that can somewhat jar in Ayr and Alloway.   The Poet lived,
worked and died in Dumfries, and is buried there, beneath the
(unnecessarily) ornate Mausoleum.   It was there, in Dumfries
and at the neighbouring farm of Ellisland, that Burns experienced
some of the greatest happiness and greatest misery of his life.   He
wrote some of his finest poetry there, too, including perhaps the
greatest of all, *'Tam o' Shanter'.*

The house in which he died, as Jean Armour gave birth to their
child, still stands, furnished as in his lifetime.   The Globe Inn still
stands, and is still a hostelry, but Anna Park, she of the golden
locks, whom Burns loved dearly, is not there now to bring a pint of
claret.

Another unique thing about Dumfries is the *camera obscura*
built in an old windmill, which also houses an interesting local
museum.   A *camera obscura* is an arrangement of lenses and
mirrors which projects an image of the outside world onto a table in
a darkened room.   By turning the lenses in different directions, it
is possible to see everything (well, almost) that is going on in the
town.   It all sounds like Big Brother Watching You, but it really is
great fun.

The old Mid-Steeple building is interesting.   It was built in
1707 as a combination of municipal buildings, court house and
jail.   There is a table of distances from various places on one of the

DUMFRIES

walls, and one distance is given to Huntingdon, in the south of England. This reminds us that cattle from all over Scotland and the islands were once driven down south in great herds to feed the population of London.

Above the doorway of Mid-Steeple there is, carved into the stone, the old Scottish measure of an *'Ell'* — 37 inches. That was the standard from which yardsticks and rulers were once made.

Lincluden Collegiate Church and Convent, sadly surrounded now by modern ugliness, is still very much worth a visit. It is said to be perhaps the best example of Decorated architecture in Scotland, and is certainly impressive. Particularly so, perhaps, is the tomb of Princess Margaret, standing under a great arch.

It was Archibald the Grim, he of Threave Castle, who turned out the Benedictine monks at the end of the 14th century, after they had enjoyed Lincluden for 200 years. He turned the monastery into a Collegiate Church.

It stands on a bend of the Cluden water, and upstream is Ellisland, Burns's farm. The banks of the Cluden Water were one of Burns's favourite walks, and he immortalised them in the superb *'Ca' the knowes'*. Tradition has it that the whole of *Tam o' Shanter* was composed in one afternoon as Burns strolled back and forth on Cluden's banks, and that, as he composed, the banks rang with his laughter at the images he was calling forth.

J.M. Barrie, although not a native of Dumfries, grew up there and attended Dumfries Academy. It is said that *Peter Pan* developed from old myths he learned at Dumfries in his youth.

Strangely, many of the Galloway myths and legends still concern small dark men who live underground and can influence us today, for good or ill. Perhaps it is some kind of folk memory of the Celts, Picts, Gaels and Brythons of long ago. This tradition was used by John Buchan in his weird and very frightening *'Watcher by the Threshold'*, a story of small people living underground to this day in Galloway.

DUMFRIES MUSEUM, Church St.
Natural and human history of Dumfries
and Galloway.   Open all year.
Admission free.
CAMERA OBSCURA,
Dumfries Museum, Church St.
1836 Astronomical instrument giving
views of the town and surrounding area.
Open April — September.
Admission: Adults 50p. Children 25p.
OLD BRIDGE HOUSE, Mill Road.
Victorian and Edwardian period rooms.
Open April — September.   Admission
Free.
BURNS HOUSE, Burns St. Poet's
home during last three years of his
life.   Open all year.
Admission: Adults 30p. Children 15p.
HOURS OF OPENING.
Mon—Sat 10am—1pm: 2pm—5pm
Sunday 2pm — 5pm.
(Closed Sun. & Mon. Oct.—March)

DUMFRIES MUSEUMS

NEW FOR 1986: **ROBERT BURNS CENTRE, MILL Rd.**
The story of Robert Burns and his life in Dumfries.   Exhibition, audio-visual theatre, shop and cafe.
Opening: April–Sept. Mon-Sat 10a.m.–8p.m. Sun 2p.m.–5p.m.
Oct.–March: Tues.–Sat. 10a.m.–1p.m. 2p.m.–5p.m.

It was in the old Gréyfriars Church of Dumfries, now long gone, that Robert Bruce, quarrelling, killed The Red Comyn, a deed that led eventually to Bruce's leadership of the Scots' struggle for independence, and to his Kingship.

South of Dumfries, on the B 725, is Caerlaverock Castle. This lies in an area remote from many of the changes of today. It cannot be very different from the times, two hundred and more years ago, when Robert Burns rode those roads, carefully not looking too closely for those who might be offending against the excise laws.

Caerlaverock was for centuries the seat of the Maxwell family. Today, ruinous, it still presents a clear picture of great power and over-weening ambition. Go there for the delight of the country-side, as well as to wander through those ruins and admire their beauty.

You will certainly derive much pleasure from the nature reserve at Caerlaverock, and especially perhaps from the great wealth of birdlife. This is a major area for flighting wildfowl, and at the right times of the year you can see great flocks of migratory birds resting on their long journey.

LINCLUDEN COLLEGE

DUNURE. If you are travelling south from Ayr by the main coast road (A719), there is a chance to see several of the most romantic ruins in all of southern Scotland. At Culzean, you can enjoy the wonders of a castle built with high art in a time of peace; at Dunure you can think about a bloody past.

About seven miles after leaving Ayr, take the minor road on the right which leads down to the coast and the utterly delightful little fishing harbour of Dunure. Not much fishing takes place from there today: the harbour mouth is silted, and the long tradition broken. Still, it is a gem of a place, and well worth the small detour to visit. The square harbour was built about one hundred years ago, and the village thrived. Nearby Pan Point commemorates the place where sea water was evaporated to obtain salt. The production of salt was once a considerable industry all along this and the Solway coast: the salt was needed to preserve the fish catch, chiefly. The discovery of the considerable coal deposits in Ayrshire made the industry thrive, since the new-found coal was used to boil the seawater in the pans. However, like the coal miners, the salt workers had a miserable life, since they were bound like serfs to their employers.

Just above, and south of the village, are the few crumbling remains of Dunure Castle, to be looked at, perhaps thought about, but not clambered over. Strangely, although the castle has crumbled, the dovecot, like some giant beehive, remains almost intact. Draw what lesson you will from that!

The castle was the home of the Kennedys, and they were one of the great families whose feuds and quarrels and greed make such sad reading today. Perhaps the most notorious Kennedy action to have taken place at Dunure was the roasting alive of the

Commendator of Crossraguel Abbey. This particularly nauseating deed was done on the order of Gilbert, 4th Earl of Cassilis. Gilbert was described by a contemporary as being *'ane wery greidy man who cairrit nocht how he got land.'*

During the Reformation in Scotland, the lands of Crossraguel Abbey, about six miles from Dunure, were appropriated, and Gilbert believed he had more right to them than anyone else. However, Queen Mary appointed one Alan Stewart as Commendator, which meant that although not owning the very extensive Crossraguel lands, Stewart had their use and profit. He enjoyed that for several years, but was one day kidnapped by Gilbert's men and taken to Dunure. There he was invited to sign over the lands, but refused to do so. Gilbert's men then stripped him, and suspended him over a fire in the vaults. Thoughtfully, he was well basted with oil, and, not surprisingly, finally agreed to sign papers transferring the lands of Crossraguel to Gilbert.

A week later the Earl, perhaps advised by some catch-penny lawyer, sent a second paper for signing, to the effect that the first had been freely given. Bravely, Alan Stewart refused to sign this, and was again given the treatment. Naturally, he again signed.

"Seeing I was in danger of my life, my flesch consumed and brunt to the bones and that I would not condescend to their purpose, I was releivit of that paine whairthrow I will never be able nor weill in my lyfetime."

It happened that Alan Stewart was brother-in-law to the neighbouring Kennedy of Bargany, and Bargany men finally rescued him from Dunure. Stewart complained to the Privy Council, but little good it did him, for even the Crown was not disposed to tangle with Gilbert, whose by-name was 'King of Carrick'. However, Gilbert was confined for a brief time in Dumbarton, and agreed to pay the crippled Alan Stewart a small pension. History does not record whether, for once, he kept his word. But he did keep the lands. In such ways were the great estates brought into being.

CROSSRAGUEL ABBEY

Sir Walter Scott used the sad story of Alan Stewart in his novel 'Ivanhoe'. There, Isaac of York was threatened with a similar roasting.

On a happier note, it is recorded that Mary, Queen of Scots, stayed as an honoured guest at Dunure Castle in 1563. It is perhaps one of the few places where that unfortunate lady was a happy and voluntary guest.

For beachcombers, the beach at Dunure is well worth combing for agates. Indeed, this is true of much of the Ayrshire coast.

Since you are in this part of the country, and have perhaps already visited two very interesting relics of the past, Culzean and Dunure Castles, you might like to round off the day by visiting two more: Baltersan Castle, and Crossraguel Abbey. They are close together, on the main road (A 77) running south from Ayr to Girvan and Stranraer.

Before you reach the main road, though you will travel up — or is it down? — the strange Electric Brae. On this short stretch of road, which is signposted, all your senses tell you that you are travelling down hill. And yet if you stop your car and then let it coast for a yard or two, you find that it goes uphill! It is a very strange sensation; an optical illusion, of course, but decidedly peculiar.

The first Romantic Ruin on the road is Baltersan Castle. Had Baltersan been placed anywhere other than close by Crossraguel Abbey, it would surely have been famous as a fine and picturesque ruin. Unfortunately, it is quite overshadowed by its neighbour, which is even finer and even more picturesque. Baltersan is well worth a visit, though, if only to see the lovely 13th century cross.

Crossraguel Abbey is roofless and magnificent. It was originally built about 1244 for the Cluniac monks, and was founded by Duncan, the 1st Earl of Carrick. It was largely rebuilt in the 15th century, after the Wars of Independence, and was used, although only by a handful of monks, until 1592, during the Reformation. Like their close relatives the Cistercians, the Cluniac monks were skilful farmers. They admitted large numbers of lay brothers to their Order, and these farmed cattle and sheep, and grew grain on a large scale. As time passed, though, and especially after the Black Death in the 14th century, the rich farms of the Abbeys ceased to have any religious significance, and became purely commercial operations.

Crossraguel was a rich foundation, and owned vast areas of land. Towns and villages for considerable distances around paid their tribute and rent to Crossraguel.   It was a rich prize when the Reformation stripped the monks of their wealth, and one can understand Gilbert's determination to acquire it.   His methods left a lot to be desired, though.

The design of Crossraguel seems to show a strong French influence.   It is long and narrow, and the gatehouse and Abbot's Tower seem more designed for defence than worship.   The huge fireplace in the kitchen could well have roasted an ox, and perhaps often did.   There is an interesting Abbot's Throne actually carved into the wall of the Chapter House.

From Crossraguel continue on the same road to Kirkoswald.

Like some other Ayrshire villages today, Kirkoswald, so far as the tourist is concerned, is notable chiefly for its association with Robert Burns.   Previously a weaving village, it was, like several others, founded by the local landed proprietors to provide employment for peasants cleared from the land during the great Agricultural Revolution of the 18th century.   In the Highlands of Scotland, the Clearances led to mass emigration, often forced: in the Lowlands, to the establishment of village and cottage industries.   But in both Highlands and Lowlands, clearances were extensive.

Although not the scene of Burns's *Tam o' Shanter,* the poem was founded upon Kirkoswald characters and a tale local to the village (although other places lay claim to it).   Tam o' Shanter himself was Douglas Graham, tenant of Shanter Hall farm. Douglas Graham was also a dealer in malt, and a part-time smuggler, using his boat, the *'Tam o' Shanter'*.   The cottage of Souter Johnny (shoemaker or cobbler) is still in Kirkoswald, and is carefully preserved.   In the garden there are statues of the two great drinkers.   The statues are by Thom, a local, self-taught, sculptor.

Blanefield House is near Kirkoswald.   That was the family home of Sir Gilbert Blane, born in 1749, and later surgeon to the

West Indies Fleet. Sir Gilbert discovered that scurvy, the scourge of sailors in those days, could be cured by drinking lime juice, and he ordered that all ships carry a supply of the juice, both as a preventative and as a cure. From that grew the name '*Limey*' still applied, usually disdainfully, to Englishmen, especially in America and Australia.

Burns himself spent some weeks in Kirkoswald in 1775, and it was probably then that he heard the tale of Tam o' Shanter. He was attending school in the village, polishing his trigonometry, and that in itself indicates what an unusual person he was, and from what an unusual family he sprang. Few youngsters then, children of small peasant farmers, got to the length of studying trigonometry.

However, by Burns's own account, he did not benefit greatly, for his lessons were disrupted by the sight of a bonny lass in a neighbouring garden. She '*upset my trigonometry, and set me off at a tangent from the sphere of my studies....The last two nights of my stay in the country, had sleep been a mortal sin, I was innocent. I returned home considerably improved.*'

The stretch of coast from Dunure to Turnberry is rich in legends of King Robert Bruce. There is little enough left of Turnberry castle today, just a ditch on the landward side and the fragments of a wall facing the sea. A lighthouse occupies what was once the courtyard of the castle, and the extraordinary, intrusive Victorian Turnberry Hotel overlooks it.

The child who was to be King of Scotland, and to free his country from English rule, was born there. That was Robert de Bruce, and the story of how he happened to be born at all is a tale, and a true one, fit for the pages of a romantic novel. It happened in 1271. Marjory, Countess of Carrick, was a young widow whose husband had been killed the previous year on a Crusade in Palestine. Marjory happened to be out riding one day in the forests near her castle of Turnberry, and met a young knight hunting. That was Robert Bruce, son of the Earl of Annandale

TURNBERRY CASTLE AND LIGHTHOUSE

and Cleveland.   Marjory took an instant liking for Robert — even fell instantly in love — and invited him to stay at her castle.

Robert demurred.   He knew that the lady was a ward of the King, and that dalliance there could be dangerous and expensive. But Marjory was insistent, and had her men surround Robert and take him off to Turnberry.   The two stayed together for fifteen days — and nights — in the castle, and then emerged to be married.   The King was indeed incensed when he learned of this, and inflicted heavy financial penalties, but the marriage seems to have been a happy one, and Robert Bruce, future King of Scotland, was born in Marjory's castle of Turnberry.   He was the first of twelve children.

Turnberry Castle was occupied by English troops when Robert and his small force landed on the mainland in 1307.   He landed close by, perhaps at Maidens, but by-passed the castle and went off into the waste of hills beyond to begin his Long March which led finally to Bannockburn and victory.

GATEHOUSE OF FLEET

GATEHOUSE OF FLEET. A fine, couthy little Scottish town, on the lovely Water of Fleet. Once, it was quite a prosperous cotton spinning and weaving town, but now industry has deserted it, leaving it quiet and rather dreamy. Cally House, now a fine hotel, was built by the Murrays of Broughton in the late 18th century, to designs by Robert Milne. It is an impressive sight, best seen perhaps, from the Creetown road. Of course, since it is an hotel, you can view it from the inside! Remember the German philosopher who said that a church is best viewed from the outside, a public house from the inside, and a mountain from the foot!

It was the Murrays who tried hard and expensively to establish the cotton industry at Gatehouse of Fleet. Like so many other Lowland landowners, they sought employment for the many peasants dispossessed during the Enclosures.

It is believed that Robert Burns wrote what is almost recognised — very rightly — as the Scottish National Anthem at the Murray Arms in Gatehouse of Fleet. It is said that he wrote *'Scots wha ha'e wi' Wallace bled'* in one night, after a storm-tossed ride from Creetown.

Sir Walter Scott 'borrowed' Gatehouse and used it in his 'Guy Mannering', calling it 'Kippletringan'.

Cardoness Castle is about a mile out of town, on the Creetown road (A 75). It is one of the finest ruins in this country of fine ruins. Roofless now, it seems to have been quite impregnable in its day. Note particularly the 'Murder Hole' above the gateway, from which boiling pitch, or anything else handy, could be poured onto attackers. The castle was built in the 15th. century by the McCullochs.

Another castle, that of Rusko, about 4 miles north-west of Gatehouse, was built in the 16th. century by the Gordons of Lochinvar, and it was from that family that Young Lochinvar came when he rode out of the West in Sir Walter Scott's poem.

Five miles south of Gatehouse of Fleet is Kirkandrews. This most peculiar village is entirely made of castles. The church, the farms, the laundry, even the pigsties, are castles. And not one is more than eighty years old. They were all built in the first decade of this century by the eccentric James Brown, a local land-owner. Even if the idea of a village of modern castles does not fascinate you, then you will be fascinated by the maze of attractive lanes, running down to the coast in that forgotten piece of country.

GIRVAN.

GIRVAN. Girvan is a quiet and pleasant place, on the main road south from Ayr to Stranraer.

It is a little town of perhaps 8000 people, but with a population much increased in the holiday season. It is the town furthest 'doon the watter' from Glasgow, and traditionally popular as the place for a seaside holiday. With long, safe, sandy beaches, gentle promenades and attractive gardens, as well as a wide range of entertainments, it is indeed the ideal holiday resort, as several generations would happily testify. The harbour is crowded with fishing boats at the weekend, and there is a good deal of pleasure boating, too. Across the harbour is a busy boat-yard, with usually one or two fishing boats on the slips for repair or overhaul.

But of course Girvan is very much more than its pretty face. The Town Charter was granted by Charles I in 1668, but the site of Girvan has been occupied since at least 5000 B.C. A Bronze-Age urnfield was discovered as late as 1961 off Coalports Lane to the east of the town, and there is a pre-historic fort at Dinvin, four miles south of the town, on the Newton Stewart Road. That fort, it is supposed, was a refuge and a defense against Norse raiders. The ruined chapel of St. Donan, two miles north of the town, was mentioned in a Charter of 1404.

As with many other places, the town was traditionally dominated — virtually owned body and soul — by Crossraguel Abbey. The town lay on the pilgrim way to Whithorn, which was one of the holiest sites in pre-Reformation Scotland. King Kenneth VI is recorded as staying at Girvan on his way to Whithorn, and so is the tragic, dying Robert Bruce, who held a court at Knockcushan in February, 1329. Bruce, in his hunting days, and in his days as a great guerilla leader, knew every nook and cranny of the hills around Girvan.

KING'S ARMS HOTEL

Dalrymple St. GIRVAN

This lovely old coaching Inn, now a 2 Star Hotel, is very central, in easy walking distance of all Girvan's many attractions.

There are **28** very comfortable bedrooms, all with H. & C., and many with private bathrooms and colour T.V.

The Coach Lamp Restaurant is justly famed for its excellent food and wine, and the three bars are friendly and well-stocked.

We specialise in all-inclusive Golf Packages, and Mini Bus and Fishing Trips can be arranged.

Ample car parking at rear of Hotel.

Tel: Girvan (0465) 3322

JAMES JOHNSTONE
Established 1922

If you are looking for good old-fashioned Scottish fare, visit us and sample something from our high-quality and extensive menu in the welcoming atmosphere of our restaurant. On leaving, you may well be tempted to purchase something from our shop, which offers a wide range of top class bakery goods and confectionery.

Restaurant Open daily to 6 p.m.
Shop closes at 5 p.m.
74 Dalrymple St. Girvan.
Tel: Girvan (0465) 2376

With the Reformation, Invergarvane, to give the town its old name, was freed from its virtual serfhood to Crossraguel, whose handful of monks had taken rents from the town. The weaving industry developed and flourished, and the old weavers' houses are still obvious, especially in the south of the town.

Girvan is in reality only a fishing village writ large, and is mainly unspoiled. As in most towns and villages of South-west Scotland, the buildings are clean and bright with colour wash. It is all a long way from the days of 200 years ago, when one traveller was unable to find shelter, and wrote that the houses were little more than holes in the ground.

There is a friendly little stumpy tower — called 'Stumpy' — at the corner by the traffic lights. It was once the town jail. Also on that corner is an aviary in the attractive small Knockcushan gardens. It is not often you get an aviary on the rates, so take advantage of it.

There is a factory just north of the town, with the rather peculiar name of Alginate Industries. It takes in Hebridian seaweed at one end and from the other ejects a strange range of products made from that seaweed. Amongst other things, seaweed appears in your jellies, jams and custard powder, and even in your beer.

Girvan, by the way, is where boat trips leave from for Ailsa Craig. And that is a trip most certainly worth taking.

GIRVAN

GLENLUCE. The village of Glenluce is a pretty place, and always worth a visit, but the great attraction there must be the Abbey.

Founded in 1190 by Roland, Lord of Galloway, it is one of Scotland's finest relics. It was a Cistercian Abbey, and was visited frequently by the Kings and Queens of Scotland, including Robert Bruce and Mary, Queen of Scots.

Excavations have uncovered not only architectural details of great beauty, but also glimpses of a whole way of life, with many kinds of tools and artifacts. Clay drain pipes have carefully moulded sockets to lock each to the next, more precisely than do the plastic products of today. There is a clay tile with the imprint of a dog's foot. One can imagine the artisan angrily cursing as he chased away the wandering cur that threatened to spoil his careful work, then looking round with fear lest some passing monk heard his curses.

The Chapter House is especially beautiful. The roof is supported by a single great pillar, with vaulting ribs to each corner. One thinks kindly of those, our ancestors, who worked with primitive tools and yet left us such haunting beauty.

In the pre-Reformation days, of course, the church and its ancilliaries literally owned much of Scotland. Some unknown old cynic wrote, of the religious orders, that:- *'They made good kail on Fridays when they fasted, and never wanted gear enough as long as their neighbours' lasted.'* The people were to a large extent serfs of the church. To be found beyond the bounds of the church which owned you was to be declared an outlaw, and that was a terrible fate. Indeed, until quite recent days, coalminers, salt workers and farm workers on lands once owned by the church, but then owned by those who acquired church lands, were themselves bound to the land, and bought and sold with it.

GLENLUCE ABBEY

With the Reformation, the church lands were broken up, and a great scramble ensued to add them to the already vast holdings of local landlords. Our old friend Gilbert, Earl of Cassillis, tried hard and successfully to get the lands of Crossraguel by foul means, and by means no less foul, tried, again successfully, to get the lands of Glenluce Abbey. He persuaded a monk to forge the signature of the Abbot on a lease of the lands. He then had the monk murdered, and proceeded to prosecute and execute the murderers for the murder he had himself instigated.

A rather happier story, not perhaps so well based on fact, concerns the 13th century wizard, Michael Scott. The district of Glenluce was vastly troubled by a plague and Michael, called in to help, lured the plague to a cellar in the Abbey, locked it in and starved it to death. However, Michael was sorely harrassed by local witches, friends of the plague, who wanted it released. So the good Michael set the witches to work making ropes from the sands of Luce Bay, and even today, if the tides are right, you can see the sand in the bay twisted into rope-like lengths as the witches continue their eternal task.

Castle Kennedy is very close to Glenluce, and certainly should be visited. Arguably, the gardens there are the finest in Scotland, and possibly the finest in Britain.

Until about a hundred years ago, the gardens were but a poor shadow of a faded glory. However, a bundle of old landscaping plans was found in a gardener's cottage during renovations, and they were the plans of the garden as it was originally. The old plans were used again, to make the gardens we view with so much delight today.

Castle Kennedy, of course, is now the seat of the Earl of Stair, and the gardens were originally planned and laid out by the second Earl, who had commanded the Scots Greys in the campaigns of the Duke of Marlborough, and who went on to become Commander in Chief of the British Army. It is said that when he retired to Castle

CASTLE KENNEDY

Kennedy, he had the trees regimented to the same plan as his troops were in at the battle of Dettingen.

Whatever the truth of that, certainly the gardens are now again restored to their former glory. Conifers of many kinds, from many countries, and rhododendrons are the most obvious beauties, but best of all, surely, are the remarkable vistas carefully designed to lead the delighted eye to glimpses of water and colour.

Lochinch Castle is in the gardens, and so are the ruins of the old Castle Kennedy. This, of course, was the very heart of the Kennedy country, almost a kingdom within a kingdom. It used to be said that:—

> *'Twixt Wigton and the town of Ayr,*
> *Port Patrick and the cruives of Cree,*
> *No man needs think for to bide there,*
> *Unless he rides wi' Kennedie.*

And it was so.

Glen App is just north of Stranraer, on the main road to Girvan. There is another delightful garden there, with quite magnificent trees and beautiful woodland glades although, sadly, it is not now open to the public.

There is a curious legend that St. Patrick once visited Glen App, but was not kindly received by the natives. They cut off his head. Not wishing to remain where he was not welcome, St. Patrick decided to return home to Ireland, and the only way was to swim. He needed to see where he was going, so he had to carry his head with him, but found swimming difficult when he carried his head in his arms. So he carried his head in his teeth, and swam all the way back to Ireland!

GLEN TROOL. If there is one place in the whole of Southwest Scotland that simply *must* be visited by the holiday-maker, then it is Glen Trool. For one thing, there is no finer view than that from the Bruce Stone there — unless it is the view from the nearby Merrick. For another thing, Glen Trool is the very womb of Scotland, from which emerged an independent nation.

The country is wild, magnificent, and very beautiful. For preference, perhaps, Glen Trool should be approached by the lonely mountain road from Straiton. That road runs under the very fingers of the Range of the Awful Hand. It is a wonderful road, and one that should be travelled anyway, even if you do not visit Glen Trool.

IN LOYAL REMEMBRANCE
OF
ROBERT the BRUCE
KING OF SCOTS
WHOSE VICTORY IN THIS
GLEN OVER AN ENGLISH
FORCE IN MARCH 1307
OPENED THE CAMPAIGN OF
INDEPENDANCE WHICH HE
BROUGHT TO A DECISIVE
CLOSE AT BANNOCKBURN
ON 24TH JUNE 1314

BRUCE STONE, GLEN TROOL

HEAD OF GLEN TROOL

The road takes you directly to Glen Trool village. The village was built for forestry workers by the Forestry Commission, and is a neat and well-kept place. Some of the cottages, no longer needed for forestry workers now that the trees are mature, are available for summer letting to visitors.

Turn left in the village, and head for Loch Trool.

At Loch Trool, you are in the middle of the Galloway Forest Park, 240 square miles of great beauty and wonderful variety. To drink most deeply of its unique beauty you must do some walking, but the Park gives great delight even to those who must confine their viewing to the windscreen of a motorcar.

At the entrance to the Glen, there is a bridge over a wild torrent of white water, with a convenient car park there. Follow the road further up the Glen to the Caldons caravan site. A stone there, allegedly carved by Old Mortality, commemorates the deaths of six Covenanters in 1685. They were surprised at their worship by a party of dragoons led by one Col. Douglas. Two of the dragoons were also killed in the fight.

112

From the car park, the road climbs up and away through the Glen, giving fascinating glimpses of the Loch below. At the last parking place on the road, leave your car, and walk the few steps to the Bruce Memorial Stone. Almost the full length of Loch Trool, in all its loveliness, lies below you. On all sides, steep hills and fells surround the winding loch, and fall clear to the water. The tiny tree-clad island in the Loch is the Maiden Isle. Across the Loch is the great sweep of Lamachan Hill. (Gaelic: *The Tawny Hill.)*

It was on that top, on a March day in 1307, that Robert Bruce placed his men, as an English army approached. As the English, on foot over the rough ground, clambered along the narrow track between the water and the hill, Bruce, according to legend, blew three great blasts on his horn, and at that signal, his men rolled great boulders down the hill, putting the invaders into disarray and killing many. The subsequent battle was a clear victory for the Scots, and began the long process leading to Bannockburn and the renewed independence of Scotland.

There are several walks well sign-posted round the Glen. It is the favourite place for beginning the climb up The Merrick, southern Scotland's highest peak. The Merrick is by no means a very severe walk, but care is essential, and proper clothing. The weather can change quickly in those hills, and mist or freezing rain can transform even the gentlest hill (and the Merrick is *not* gentle) into a real obstacle.

In the days before the Forestry Commission took over the land around Glen Trool, sheep were the sole crop of those gaunt hills. It is recorded that a local shepherd once told Lord Boyd-Orr that: 'Ony sauchle o' a body can write a book, but it tak's a man to herd The Merrick.' Certainly, to shepherd those hills was a demanding job, and the hill shepherd a dedicated person, whose task really was — and is — hard, harsh and lonely.

If you are not a walker, do at least go on the track past the Bruce Memorial Stone down to the bridge over the Buchan Burn.   If the Burn is in spate, the torrent above and below the bridge is a mass of roaring white water.   The inscription on the bridge — rapidly and sadly disappearing now — is from the poem by Sir Walter Scott.

Look out for wild goats hereabouts — although these 'wild' goats have learned that visitors' sandwiches are a useful source of extra food!

BUCHAN FALLS, GLEN TROOL

KIRKCUDBRIGHT. This wholly delightful small town was originally the kirk of St. Cuthbert. At least, that is what one theory holds: there are several others. In any case, after changing many times over the centuries, the name is currently pronounced 'Kir-coo-bree'.

There are so many delights in and around Kirkcudbright that it is difficult to know how to begin describing them. First, perhaps, is the sheer attractiveness of the town. It is neat, well-ordered and pretty — as is a well-kept garden. Over everything there is a wonderful clarity of light that has attracted artists for many years. It is, indeed, the sort of light that seems to intensify all colours, not wash them out. It is the sort of light that attracts painters to Newlyn and St. Ives in England, and to Arles in France.

The old, dreaming buildings in the town, the Tolbooth, the Castle and the wynds and closes, give Kirkcudbright a timeless air. Fortunately, 'Town Planning' and 'modernisation' hardly intrude, although that is not so say that you can't find the sort of food, drink and accommodation we have all been led to expect these days.

The High Street is particularly fascinating. 'L' shaped, it includes many old style Scottish and even Georgian buildings. The old Tolbooth is at the corner, and it was there that John Paul Jones, founder of the American navy and leader of several daring raids on Scotland during the American War of Independence, was once briefly imprisoned. He was charged with the murder of a crew member during the time he was captain of a merchant ship. John Paul Jones was of course a Scot, born in 1744 at Kirkbean, 12 miles south of Dumfries. It was perhaps a litle odd that John Paul Jones raided Scotland so much, for by-and-large Scotland strongly supported the cause of the American colonists against the English.

MACCELLAN'S CASTLE

It is not generally known that as well as being the 'Father of the American Navy', John Paul Jones was also, in a sense, the Father of the Russian Navy. Rather ironic, in the light of later events! It happened that Empress Catherine the Great of Russia called for Capt. Jones to help Russia in war against the Turks. She said that she was *'waiting for him from day to day.'* In the light of what is now known about her character and proclivities, one might well wonder for what she was waiting. In any case, Capt. Jones, who seemed to be as keen as she was, and who happened to be in Sweden when the call came for him, made a quite mad dash into Russia across the icy Gulf of Bothnia, threatening his crew with his

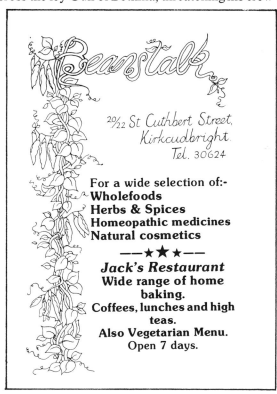

pistol when they protested at the risks.   It was probably worth it, though, for within a very short time he became a Russian rear-admiral.   Four years later, he died, alone and in poverty, in Paris.

There are many delightful stories about Capt. Jones.   One concerns his raid on St. Mary's Isle, just off Kirkcudbright.   In April 1778, Capt. Jones, in a frigate disguised as a merchant ship, landed 40 men there in an attempt to kidnap the Earl of Selkirk, who was active in opposing the American cause, and who, it was intended, was to be a hostage for American prisoners.   John Paul Jones had once been a garden boy at Arbigland, those delightful gardens near the Earl's estate, and so knew the area well.

It happened that the Earl was not at home, so the raiders, as raiders always do, did a little private looting, and carried off the Earl's silver plate.   This upset the always-chivalrous Capt. Jones, and he promised to return the plate when possible.   Six years later he did so, and the tea leaves were still in the pot, so well had John Paul Jones looked after the loot.   Indeed, the tea leaves are still there to this day.

Look at the old market cross, now set into a wall above the Town Well, and look, too, at the iron jougs chained to the wall there.   Those iron collars held many a citizen who had offended the Kirk or State.   Be thankful those days are past.

Burns, who knew Kirkcudbright well, composed the Selkirk Grace while staying at the Selkirk Arms there.   That little stanza is all that many people know of Burns.   And while on the subject of grace, and food, do try some 'queenies' while in Kirkcudbright — or anywhere else along the Solway coast.   These little scallop-like fish are a great gastronomic delight, and yet are but little known.

Maclellan's Castle, a 16th. century tower-house, was built by Sir Thomas Maclellan, chiefly with stones from the ruinous Greyfriars Monastery nearby.   At that time, it was not necessary to build a fortified house, so that the castle is in fact a fine example

KIRKCUDBRIGHT HARBOUR

of Scottish domestic architecture. Particularly interesting is the Great Hall, and the enormous lintel over the fireplace, cut from a single stone. There is a spy hole in the lintel, and a small room behind it. One wonders what devious plotting went on to make that necessary.

The castle faces Greyfriars Church, an even older building, and nearby is the Stewartry Museum. The museum is another example of the small regional collections, organised by local people, that are playing such an important part in preserving the past for us today, and for the future. The exhibits are local things, many of them not so old, but no longer in use today, and very evocative of the life and times of our parents and grandparents — not of our distant ancestors. Indeed, there can be no better way of getting a feeling and understanding of Kirkcudbright today, than spending time in this little museum, where the immediate past is brought into focus.

By all means also visit Broughton House, which the painter E.A. Hornel bequeathed to the town. As well as many of Hornel's paintings, which show clearly his impressionistic style, especially in the paintings of children, there is his magnificent library, and a whole host of lovely articles collected throughout his life.

Dundrennan Abbey is just a few miles east of Kirkcudbright, by the A711. This 12th century Cistercian Abbey, a very venerable and stately ruin, is where Mary, Queen of Scots, spent her last night in her realm, before leaving — poor self-deluded woman — for England and her death.

Dundrennan was a Cistercian Abbey founded in 1142, but, after the Reformation, much of it was demolished, and today a good deal of the little village of Dundrennan is built from the Abbey stones. But quite enough remains to make a ruin of great beauty and splendour. Quite certainly a place that should not be missed.

KIRKMICHAEL. Lying on the B7045 between Straiton and Ayr, Kirkmichael is another of those tidy, wide-streeted villages of which Ayrshire has so many, and which delight all visitors. You might think that it is pretty enough, and give it a word of praise as you drive through. It really would be a pity to go straight through, though, and not stop at the old Churchyard.

There is a very interesting gravestone there, marking the resting place of yet another Covenanter. The whole of South-west Scotland has these in sad plenty: this one is rather different.

To begin with, it is not the usual simple headstone. This is a large and elaborate monument. Let into the monument is a much older stone, the original headstone.

The inscription on the headstone reads:
> *Here lyes Gilbert McAdam who was shot in this parish*
> *By the Laird of Colzean and Ballochmil.*
> *For his adherence to the Word of God and*
> *Scotland's Covenanted work of Reformation.*

Look at it, and it is quite clear that the second line has at some time been effaced and then later recut. The story is interesting.

It all happened in 1685, the Killing Year, when so many people died so horribly for their faith. Gilbert McAdam was one of them. Earlier, in 1682, Gilbert had been arrested for refusing to go to church, where the services were conducted by one of those King's Curates appointed against the wishes and beliefs of the Congregation. He was sent for trial at Dumfries, but escaped. The soldiers soon caught him though, and he was sentenced to transportation to America, as a plantation slave. Death might have been better.

KIRKMICHAEL GRAVEYARD

Negroes were not the first slaves in America — British convicts were, and their crime might have been no more than the theft of a loaf, or worshipping in their own way.   Children, women and men were shipped to labour in slavery, if they survived the awful journey.   A monument in nearby Maybole records the names of six men of Maybole who drowned when one such slave ship foundered in a gale.   Altogether fifty-seven Covenanters from Ayrshire perished in that one ship, and there were other similar tragedies.

Gilbert McAdam survived the journey, and was duly sold into slavery.   Somehow, though, his father raised enough money to buy his freedom, and Gilbert returned to Scotland, as strong as ever in his beliefs.

It was in June 1685 that he went to a prayer meeting in Kirkmichael, and was surprised there by a party of soldiers led by Sir Archibald Kennedy of Culzean and John Reid of Ballochmyle. The prayer meetings, held in cottages all over the county, were highly illegal, since worship outside the authorised churches was a capital offence. It is said that Gilbert McAdam was trying to shield his mother when the fatal shots were fired. In any case, Gilbert was dead, and his mother cursed those responsible, especially the Kennedy family. And the curse may have been successful, for there is a legend that the Devil himself was seen driving a coach-and-four over a stormy sea to collect the soul of Archibald Kennedy.

Gilbert was buried in the churchyard, and the first stone erected over his head. That was not the end of the story, for in due time came the restoration of Presbyterianism in Scotland. Many changed sides with their religious beliefs then, including the Laird of Ballochmyle, John Reid. So successfully did Reid change that he was appointed an elder of his church. But he was haunted by that line on Gilbert McAdam's gravestone. It recorded an episode he wanted to forget, and perhaps sincerely regretted. So one dark night a few minutes' work with hammer and chisel obliterated the record of who was responsible for Gilbert McAdam's death.

Facts, though, are stubborn things. There were those who were determined that the facts about Gilbert McAdam's death should not be obliterated, and on another dark night, the shaming words were again cut into the headstone, it is said by Old Mortality himself, Robert Paterson, and there you can see them today.

It all seems long ago now, not only in time but in character. Today, people can hardly be persuaded to vote for their beliefs, let alone die for them. Perhaps in another three hundred years people will wonder about our lack of faith just as we wonder at the readiness of our ancestors three hundred years ago to die for matters we think of no consequence.

MAYBOLE. This is a cramped and traffic-choked little town just south of Ayr, but well worth a visit, if only to see the two 'castles' which grace the main street. They were in fact town houses, and remind us that in its day, Maybole was the centre of a cultivated and prosperous society. That day came, of course, when the local chiefs ceased their ancient and bloody feuding, and settled down to exploit the lands they had acquired. Maybole was then indeed the capital of Carrick.

One castle, the Tolbooth Tower, is now in public use, and was once the town house of Kennedy of Blairquhan. The other, still known as Maybole Castle, is in private occupation. It was the town house of the Earl of Cassillis, leader of the Kennedys. Built early in the 17th century, when craftsmanship and artistry were finally coming together in a country more settled and peaceful than before, it is a very handsome building indeed. The heads carved round the tower are linked with the tale of a Kennedy countess carried off by a band of gypsies. If the old folk ballad is to be believed, she was not unwilling to go. However, the Earl and his men caught up with them, and Johnny Faa and his band were hanged, and the lady returned to the arms of her husband. I wonder. The heads, it is said, were carved on the stones to remind the lady of her misdeeds.

In John Knox street there is the house where, in 1561, Quentin Kennedy and John Knox disputed publicly for three days over whether the bread and wine offered by Melchizadec to Abraham constituted a Mass. Of such *minutae* are religious bigotries made.

On a less gloomy note, it was at a fair in Maybole that William Burnes met the lass who was to be the mother of Robert Burns. Agnes Broun was a farmer's daughter when she married William Burnes. Her first-born, Robert, was later to recall that the songs she so often sang so sweetly fired his love of Scottish song. She had learned those songs in Maybole. Later, as the grinding poverty and toil of life as the wife of a small tenant farmer destroyed her gaiety, she was to sing less and less.   Robert noted this, and was angered by the reasons for it.

MAYBOLE CASTLE

MACCLURGS' GRAVESTONE, MINIGAFF

MINIGAFF. Today, Minigaff seems to be little more than a pleasant suburb of Newton Stewart, but it was not always so. Long before Newton Stewart was thought of, Minigaff was a bustling place and the market town for the district. The name, incidentally, derives from the Gaelic *Monadh-dubh*, and means 'a dark, mountainous region.' It must surely refer to the hills to the north.

No area in the whole of this land can be so rich in prehistoric remains as Minigaff is — and the whole area covered by this book is rich in such relics of the distant past. Cairns, standing stones, stone circles and motes seem to be everywhere in this parish. The De'il's Dyke runs hereabouts, and many of the relics are near to it, although which came first, the relics or the Dyke, it would be difficult to say.

It is impossible to recommend any particular one of those many standing stones and circles as being *the* one to visit, but the two weird standing stones known as The Thieves always make a deep impression on everyone who visits them. They are two great blocks of whinstone, one triangular and one rectangular, the first 6 feet 8 inches high, the other 7 feet 4 inches, surrounded by the remnants of an oval rubble wall 30 feet long. They stand — they have stood for 4000 years — about 5 miles north-west of Minigaff, just beyond Cumloden. The De'il's Dyke is close by.

In the old churchyard of Minigaff is a headstone of the MacClurg family, showing their coat of arms. It depicts a raven transfixed by an arrow, and beneath it, two more ravens transfixed by a single arrow. The story behind it is that on the eve of the battle of Raploch Moor, Robert Bruce stayed the night at a little cottage by Clatteringshaws Loch. (At least, today it is a loch: then it was but a stream.) The lady of the house asked of Bruce that her three sons might join him. Surely as a jest, for he needed every man he could find, the king said that first they must show their skill with their bows. The first shot at a raven, and missed altogether. The second shot, and killed the raven.   The third shot, and killed two ravens with one arrow.

The three young men joined Bruce, and it is said that it was they who organised the Phantom Army, by fixing pieces of rattling metal to the backs of every animal — horse, sheep, goat and cow — that they could find, and driving them in the darkness over the moors, so that the English, hearing the rattle of metal, thought they were facing a much bigger army than Bruce's little band.

MONIAIVE   Maxwellton Braes, where Bonny Annie Laurie loved and was loved, lie north-west of Dumfries — although not at Maxwelltown, the Dumfries suburb.   Maxwellton Braes are near Moniaive, on the lovely B729 road from Dumfries to Carsphairn. Moniaive is a delightful village (a winner of the 'Britain In Bloom' contest).

Annie Laurie's lover, so he said himself, would have laid down and died for her.   But was it true?   The fact is that when he realised his love was hopeless, he immediately went off and married someone else.   And so did Annie Laurie.   This all happened in 1694, when William Douglas of Fingland retired from the army and settled down at home.   He promptly fell in love with Annie Laurie, but her parents objected to the match, and, in the good old fashioned way, locked Annie in her room until she promised to give up her love.   This she soon did, and William went off and married another young lady, and Annie married Alexander Fergusson of Craigdarroch.   So much for his *"I'll lay me doon an' dee"*!

But he did write that wonderful love song — even though many today think that Burns wrote it.   However, the words we sing are not all his: they have been 'improved' by another of those who seek only too often to 'improve' the work of poets — and invariably all they do is pander to the 'good taste' of their own generation and class.

Craigdarroch House is still there, and still occupied.   It is a lovely old rose-pink house, and can be seen about 2 miles from the village on the Ayr road.

Maxwellton House, where Annie lived and temporarily loved, is one of the most delightful places in the whole area, and very much worth a visit. It is open to the public, but the opening hours are somewhat erratic (after all, it is still a private dwelling), so it is advisable to telephone before visiting.

Moniaive is a grand moorland village, at the foot of three lovely glens, down which tumble the three burns which join at the village to make the river Cairn. Indeed, the whole area is known as Glencairn.

The George is a fine and quite unspoiled 16th cent. Inn, complete with stone-flagged bar and smoke-darkened beams. Even the fireplace is original, and still has its traditional 'lunkie hole' where odd coins were placed (they still are) for the use of needy travellers.

This was Covenanting country, of course, and the George was the scene of many Covenanting gatherings in those past and bitter days. There is a tiny secret room built into the stairway, with a spyhole from which watch was kept for approaching Redcoats. It was not always successful, and some Covenanters were caught and killed hereabout. There is a monument to one of them just half a mile out of the village on the Carsphairn road. This is the Renwick Monument, and may well be one of those first erected by Old Mortality himself.

MULL OF GALLOWAY.   This long, narrow peninsula, running almost 20 miles south from Stranraer, is certainly one of the most interesting and beautiful areas in the whole of South-west Scotland.   It is peaceful and serene, seeming to be almost untouched by the Twentieth Century.   For the holiday maker who is seeking peace and serenity (and who is not?) it is ideal.   Port Logan, of course is there, and Port Patrick.   Both are truly delightful places, and it would be difficult to choose between them.   Fortunately that is not necessary, because only a few miles of quite empty road separate them.

The two ports both face the Atlantic's power, and that power is very clear from the great mass of broken granite and concrete slabs at the entrance to Port Patrick's tiny harbour.   At the beginning of the last century, there were plans to build a great harbour there, for the sea trade to Ireland and beyond.   However, after the enormous — for those days — sum of half a million pounds had been spent, a great Atlantic storm blew up and totally demolished the half-built harbour.   Work was never resumed, and Stranraer and Loch Ryan, more sheltered places, became the gateways to Ireland.

In the days when Port Patrick was the major port for Ireland, the village became a sort of Gretna Green for loving (or troubled) couples from Northern Ireland.   They could come over on Saturday, have their banns called on Sunday, and marry on Monday.   And presumably return to Donagadhee and their wrathful parents on Tuesday.

South from Port Logan, on Luce Bay, is the most southerly village in Scotland, Drummore, and it is a lovely, idyllic place. Three miles south again, and there is the Mull itself, a great castle-like headland, tremendous, awe-inspiring.

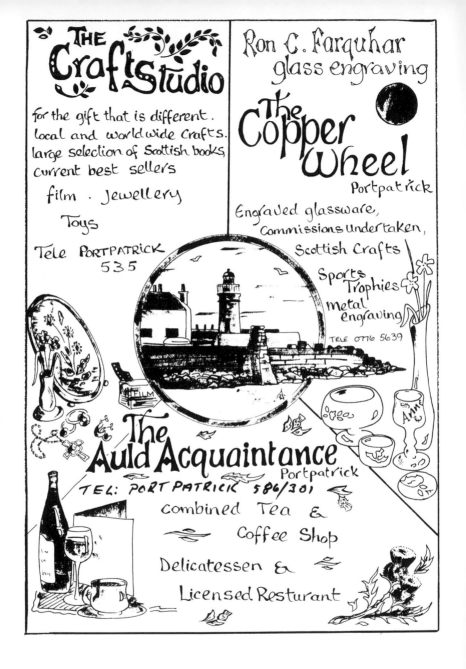

Nearby are East and West Tarbert, within a minute's walk of each other. East Tarbert, on Luce Bay, is a place of grassy cliffs and sheltered, quiet beaches. . West Tarbert faces the Atlantic, and the cliffs are steep and bare. The name 'Tarbert' is from Gaelic, and here as always, means a narrow neck of land, a place where once boats were dragged overland to avoid a dangerous sea passage. One can well imagine the sailors and fishermen, pirates and warriors of old, facing the task of dragging their boats over a few hundred yards of land rather than face the terrors of rounding the ferocious Mull.

St. Medan's cave, half a mile north of East Tarbert, is near the few pathetic ruins of the saint's chapel. The chapel is the oldest sacred building in the whole of Galloway, that land of sacred buildings. It is said that St. Medan crossed the sea from Ireland on a floating rock, and landed at Port William. She left Ireland, apparently, to escape the unwanted attentions of a too ardent lover, but she left only after plucking out her own eyes and throwing them at the feet of the no doubt greatly surprised man. However, when she landed in Scotland, at Monreith, her sight was miraculously restored by the waters of a well, a well which in later centuries became well-known as having the powers of healing. Of course it would, wouldn't it?

Almost at the tip of the Mull is Double Dykes, believed to have been the Picts' last line of defence against the Scots. It was there that Trost of the Long Knife perished, taking with him the secret of Heather Ale. A pity.

> From the bonny bells of heather,
> They brewed a drink lang-syne,
> Was sweeter far than honey,
> Was stronger far than wine.

No use repining, I suppose; it has been gone more than 1500 years now.

At the very tip of the Mull is the lighthouse, built in 1828, itself

ST. MEDAN'S CHAPEL AND MULL OF GALLOWAY

60 feet high, and standing on the 200 feet high cliff.   This is a wild place, a place of gales and thundering seas.   Yet on a summer day it can be a place of unparalleled enchantment, like most such headlands challenging those great waters.   Fortunately, this massive headland lives up to all expectations of what it should be.   There is no litter of tea rooms, no clutter of chalets.   Its bare austerity is yet unspoiled.   A great contrast to, say, Lands End.

It is said that on a clear day you could see seven Kingdoms from the end of the Mull — well, you could in the past, anyway.   They were: Scotland, Ireland, England, Wales, the Isle of Man, Strathclyde and Heaven.   They don't all exist today.

Going north again, just by Sandhead on Luce Bay, are the Kirkmadrine Stones.   These are three of the earliest and most mysterious Christian symbols in Britain — if, indeed, they are Christian at all.   Dating from the 5th or 6th Century, they carry curious symbols, whose significance and meaning is even today not fully understood.

PORT PATRICK

NEW ABBEY. Five miles south of Dumfries, on the A 710, at the village of New Abbey, is one of the most romantic and best-known ruins in all of Scotland. The little village of New Abbey nestles under the bulk of Criffel, but even Criffel seems somehow to be dominated by the ruins of the Abbey, which is popularly and delightfully known as Sweetheart Abbey.

The Abbey is a grand red ruin, founded in 1275, and called New Abbey to distinguish it from the older Dundrennan.

There is no reason to doubt the truth of the old story of its founding. It seems that Devorgilla, a young lady from a rich and powerful family, married John Balliol, also from a rich and powerful family. Devorgillla was born about 1210 at Kenmore in Galloway. Her father was Alan, last of the Kings of Galloway, and Constable of Scotland. She married when she was twenty. Both young people inherited considerable property in Scotland, England and France, and the marriage seems to have been immensely profitable, as well as romantic. Their son was also John Balliol, later King of Scotland, and a miserable King he was.

John Balliol, father, not son, was a man of wealth, influence and power, but he somehow quarrelled with the even more influential Bishop of Durham. (Balliol's main seat was at Barnard Castle, not far from Durham.) In those days, nobody, but nobody, quarrelled with a Prince of the Church, for they were less than half priests, and more than half warrior chieftains. It seems that Balliol was in the wrong in that quarrel, and certainly he had picked the wrong antagonist. The King himself ordered him to make amends, and not only was he soundly thrashed by the Bishop, but he had to establish a kind of students' hostel in Oxford, and give poor students a grant to live and study there.

SWEETHEART ABBEY

John died in 1248, leaving Devorgilla both very rich and very desolate.   She had her husband's heart embalmed, and ever afterwards carried it with her in a casket.

In her widowhood, she converted the Oxford students' hostel into a College, Balliol, of the University, and founded several religious houses, including New Abbey.   She survived John Balliol by 21 years, and when she died, aged 80, at Barnard Castle, she, and her husband's heart, were buried together beneath the High Altar of New Abbey, which became known, obviously, as Sweetheart Abbey, or, more properly perhaps, as *Dulce Cor.*   As a contemporary chronicler wrote, '*She was right pleasant and beautiful.*'

It is a touching story, and one that comes down to us over the centuries as a brief flicker of humanity and tenderness from an age better known for its brutality and inhumanity.

WEST END OF SWEETHEART ABBEY

Much remains today of the Abbey, and it is one of Britain's grandest Christian relics. It is of Early English architecture, and there are later Decorated additions. The tower still stands, and a fine West Wall, complete with three lancet windows and a wheel window above them. It was a Cistercian foundation, and the walls once enclosed thirty acres of rich cultivated land.

There is also a restored corn mill in New Abbey village, and that is an interesting place. Not so long ago, every village had its own mill, but most of them have gone now. This one has been rebuilt, and the machinery is still there as it was years ago.

This particular mill dates back to the 16th cent., and so well has it been restored that in 1984 it received the highest awards from The Civic Trust. It was semi-derelict until a few years ago — it had ceased operating in 1945 — but then restoration work was started by Mr. Stewart, the local proprietor. It was so successful that Mr. Stewart received proper recognition during the European Architectural Heritage Year.

Certainly a visit to the village of New Abbey is highly recommended, not only for the tranquil loveliness of Sweetheart Abbey, but also for a most illuminating glimpse into the past at the Corn Mill and the nearby Museum of Costume.

The great granite bulk of Criffel dominates the landscape hereabouts. It is no mountain — being a mere pimple of 1880 feet — but because its feet are right on the sea, it seems to be an impressive height. See it after rain, and there is one area where there is an outcrop of quartzite which shines so brilliantly that it is known locally as 'The Diamond.'

Getting to the top is not difficult, just a good walk, but it is very rewarding. The views are quite exceptional, from Carlisle and the Cumberland coast, down to the Lakeland hills, and across the Solway again to all the hills of the Border and southern Scotland.

Loch Kindar, between Criffel and Sweetheart Abbey, and very

SWEETHEART ABBEY

142

close to the road, is very much worth walking round.   There are two small islands in the loch, one with a ruined church on it, and the other is in fact an artificial island, a *crannog* built in the old days as a settlement and fortress.

The Cistercian monks of New Abbey once ran their vast sheep flocks over all of this land and over the slopes of Criffel.

If you can arrange it, try to be on top of Criffel when the tide is running fast over the sands of the Solway.   Watching the sea coming in as fast as it does there is an enthralling experience, and will certainly teach you to be careful about walking the Solway Sands.

On a very different note, a visit to Shambellie House, a museum of costume, is very interesting.   It lies only a quarter mile from the village of New Abbey.

Shambellie House is part of the Royal Scottish Museum, and it contains a collection of two hundred years of European fashionable dress.   It is fascinating to see how fashions have developed over that period.   It was not only hemlines that moved up and down, it was also busts, bellies and bottoms!   And why, one must wonder, did men cease, perhaps only temporarily, from being the exhibitionists that they once were.

A very interesting place indeed.

Incidentally, it was the same Mr. Stewart who renovated the Corn Mill and donated this remarkable collection.

NEW GALLOWAY. This small town for long prided itself on being the smallest Royal Burgh in Scotland, with a Charter granted by Charles I. Since the re-organisation of local government in Scotland, it is no longer a Royal Burgh, but just don't mention that around the town!

Once dominated by the vast Kenmure Castle, home of the Gordon family of Lochinvar, it is an attractive little town now, and the Castle a roofless shell. Still, the castle ruins are impressive. Of 16th century construction, the structure is 'L' shaped, on a mound above the Water of Ken. The town is a fine centre for walking or fishing. The golf course, though, is difficult to play because the views from there are quite stupendous, and more than enough to put anyone off their game!

For many holiday makers, New Galloway is no more than the end of the magnificent road from Newton Stewart, through the Galloway Forest Park. However, it is a fine little place in its own right, and well worth a visit.

Perhaps the best reason for spending time in New Galloway is the churchyard of the Church of Kells, just west of the Royal Burgh. Here there is a quite fantastic collection of tombstones, all strange epitaphs and curious carvings. One has all the equipment of a huntsman carved on it — a gun and powder horn, a fishing rod, a gun dog and a grouse. There is also a highly amusing epitaph, which you should decipher for yourself.

Another stone shows Adam and Eve, beside the Tree of Knowledge, with the serpent coiled round it. There is a wealth of carving and decoration and another curious epitaph.

Churchyards might normally be gloomy places, but this one is a fine and amusing place to spend an hour.

New Galloway lies at one end of what surely is the most spectacular road in the whole of South-west Scotland, and Newton Stewart lies at the other. That road takes you through the wild and lovely Galloway Forest Park. Most of the road (A712) runs through Forestry Commission land, but even the very intensive conifer plantations cannot mask the rugged beauty. Indeed, often the planting serves to emphasise the grandeur of the hills.

The road from New Galloway climbs up to Clatteringshaws Loch. This is an artificial loch, formed by the impounding of the river Dee. However, it has been there long enough now for the scars to have disappeared, and it sits romantically enough amongst the hills. The waters of the loch now drive turbines to generate electricity. A stop at the Deer Museum is worthwhile. In spite of the name, the museum is not concerned with deer only, although deer are very interesting, but also has excellent exhibits on the history and life of the region. In particular, there is a reconstructed Bronze Age house, discovered during work on the dam.

And if you don't stop for the Deer Museum, then you must stop for the nearby Bruce's Stone. The view to the west from there is particularly fine. Bruce, perhaps, thought so, for he is said to have rested there during the great battle fought on the Moss of Raploch close by, where the English army was defeated in 1307.

On further, and you reach The Grey Mare's Tail, a fine waterfall. This, too, is a good place to halt, because as well as the waterfall, there is a Wild Goat Park. The goats, which roamed the hills long before the Forestry Commission appeared, have been rounded up and confined to a large hillside to prevent them from damaging the young trees. It must be admitted that the goats don't seem to mind, and it lets the visitor have a close view of them and their games.

The monument close by, on the top of the knoll, is to the memory of Professor Alex. Murray, a local 'lad o' pairts' who made good in the 18th century as Professor of Oriental languages.

From the Grey Mare's Tail, continue through the conifers and larch of the Kirroughtree Forest to Minigaff (a small village with a lovely church) and Newton Stewart.

If you want to see even more of this wild and lovely country, then follow The Raiders' Road, which takes off from the main Newton Stewart road just by Clatteringshaws Dam. This is a Forestry Commission road, and they make a small charge for using it, but it does run through some remarkable and wild country. The name commemorates the route said to have been taken by the cattle raiders in Crockett's novel '*The Raiders*'. The Raiders' Road follows the Black Water of Dee down to Loch Stroan, and finally to the A762 near Loch Ken. It is very much worth the fifty pence charged for its use.

NEWTON STEWART

148

NEWTON STEWART. This is a fine little market town, and an excellent holiday centre. It is not that so much *happens* in Newton Stewart, but rather that you can do so much around there.

The town lies on the banks of 'the silv'ry winding Cree', as the song (Galloway's National Anthem!) has it. It is near to the hills, and near enough to the coast. There is hill walking and gentle strolls, if that is what you seek.

NEWTON STEWART

You enter Newton Stewart from New Galloway by a fine old bridge crossing the River Cree. To your right, the old houses on the banks of the river drop straight down to the water, just as they do in Venice. Some of the grandest views in all of Galloway can be seen from Newton Stewart and thereabouts. You can look across a green belt of rich pasture lands to the wildness of the far hills. There are soft and gentle slopes, of Craignelder and Cairnsmore of Fleet, and the higher wilderness of The Merrick and its range. Burns often walked along the banks of the Cree, and you could do much worse than that.

Newton Stewart has one of the finest small museums you will find anywhere. It is a private venture, and deserves every possible support. Go there to see the household articles, tools and farm implements of a few generations ago. Go there and surely you will say 'I watched my parents using one of those when I was a child.' Go there, in other words, for a bout of healthy nostalgia for a past that grows increasingly attractive.

Also while in Newton Stewart you would do well to visit the Glen Cree Mill. This is a large weaving factory (always fascinating), which has had the good sense to organise daily tours. Very much worth while — and it's free!

PORT LOGAN.   If anyone needed an excuse to visit the Mull of Galloway, Port Logan would provide it.   Two-thirds of the way down the Mull, on the west side, Port Logan is a veritable gem of a place.   And it is quiet, peaceful and unspoiled — like most of the Mull.

Wide open to the pounding of the Atlantic, Port Logan is only a mile from the sheltered waters of Luce Bay on the eastern side of the Mull.   You can sometimes sit on the great quiet beaches of Luce Bay, with a quiet sea before you, and hear the roar of breakers from the other side of the Mull.

But the greatest attraction of Port Logan is the Botanic Gardens.   These are, in fact, an annexe of the Royal Botanic Garden in Edinburgh, and are operated as a study and scientific centre by the Department of Agriculture and Fisheries for Scotland.   However, they are open to the public.   They are large enough to make for a full day's intense pleasure, especially if your taste is for the exotic.

There are two sections, the Walled Garden and the Woodland Garden, and each holds its wonders.   There are cabbage palms, tree ferns, eucalyptus trees, passion flowers, most remarkable rhododendrons and a great host of other lovely strangers, most of them beauties from Australasia and South America.   Altogether, a most remarkable collection, growing and thriving in a way that says much about the climate of South-west Scotland.   Not to mention the skill of the gardeners.

Do visit the gardens.   And even if it should be a wet day, you could have the unusual experience of sheltering under the leaves of a Brazilian tree growing in Gunnera Bog.   Those leaves are six feet across, and there are no bigger in Britain.

There are the ruins of Balzieland Old Castle, too, romantic and beautiful.   You approach up a stone staircase flanked by palm trees, and not many castles in Britain have *that* sort of approach!

There is a lagoon, full of goldfish (well, carp, actually) and water flowers, and great trees running down to the beach. The castle, dating back to mediaeval times, was the seat of the McDoualls of Logan.

And, of course, also in Port Logan, there is the fish pond, perhaps unique in all of Britain. This great basin, cut out of the natural stone, holds tame sea fish, great cod mostly, who come to the edge to be fed from the hands of their keeper. Skilfully designed to fill with sea water at certain tides, the pond was originally designed as a means of ensuring fresh fish all the year round. It was perhaps the first example of sea fish farming in this country.

Port Logan is, altogether, a most satisfying experience.

153

ST JOHN'S TOWN OF DALRY. When travelling north on the A 713 from Castle Douglas to Carsphairn, you first run all the way up the shore of the attractive Loch Ken.

After that, skirting New Galloway on this occasion, you soon reach the fine little St. John's Town of Dalry. There, if you go to the top of the village, you will find an ancient block of stone in the form of a chair. Sit there, and savour the legend that says John the Baptist also sat and rested in that place. If indeed he did, then he looked upon a prospect very lovely. Apart from the view of the village — which is well worth a long look, as the street runs down to the river Ken — the sky-line is the spectacular Rhinns of Kells, from Meaul to Meikle Millyea, with Corserine in the middle. Do stop and look.

From St. John's Town of Dalry, you can continue on the road to Carsphairn and Loch Doon on the main road, or, perhaps better, you can divert to the right on to B 7000 and B 729, and travel on country roads which are even quieter, to the pretty little Loch Kendoon and on to Carsphairn.

STRAITON. Straiton is a Conservation Village, and a delightful one. It lies on the east bank of the Water of Girvan, and from whichever way you approach the village, the road passes between fine whale-back hills and majestic woods. The village itself is invariably clean and neat, and is locally famous for the very colourful displays of flowers in front of every immaculate colour-washed cottage. The fine old church of St. Cuthbert contains a pre-Reformation chantry of about 1350. The main street of the village was built around 1760 by the Earl of Cassillis to lead up to the gate of the Manse.

Like so many others, it was a weaving village, established to absorb the peasants dispossessed of their holdings when the land was enclosed during the Agricultural Revolution. In the Highlands, the dispossessed were shipped like sheep to the colonies; in the Lowlands they were, by and large, trained to be weavers. And that is strange, for it was in the Lowlands that active and armed resistance was made to the enclosures and the clearances. As well as weaving, though, Straiton was a noted centre for the smuggling trade, in the past one of Ayrshire's great and thriving industries.

Straiton must also have been a centre for some doughty drinking, for in 1791 there were six inns for the 186 inhabitants of the village.

Robert Burns knew Straiton well, and in turn was well known in the Black Bull there. If he went back there now he would find it little changed from his day, even if there are few calls now for pints of claret or Lowland Malt whisky.

The prominent monument, high on a hill above the village, is to Col. James Hunter-Blair, Scots Guards, who was killed at the battle of Inkerman. How many people today could explain why that battle was ever fought, and why Col. James, and many another, had to die?

South-west of Straiton, on Glenalla Fell, there are very interesting relics of a most ancient community. Eighteen turf houses, two hut circles and a turf dyke eight feet high are still visible. It is known that these are Stone-age dwellings, but nothing else seems to be known about them.

The hill road from Straiton to Dalmellington (B741) travels over wild and bleak moors, supporting only a few sheep and a handful of very hardy cattle. Just the same, some of those sheep are the finest in the land, and if you are lucky, you just might glimpse a ram worth many thousands of pounds.

On a summer afternoon, with perhaps a curlew crying and a lark pouring out its song from high above, this moor can be a place of great peace and loneliness.

The hill road from Straiton to Newton Stewart is one of the finest

in all of South-west Scotland.   It begins quietly enough, running along a peaceful and fruitful valley, but then begins its climb into the wildness of the hills.

William Neill, a fine local poet of the present day, wrote:
On the far side of Straiton, on the hill road
The farm names change to Gaelic.
So does the country, bare moorland with no fences,
the rock teeth tearing at the base of clouds.

He has caught it exactly, for it *is* wild country, and exciting, a road to be lingered over and cherished.

STRAITON

157

ROAD BEYOND STRAITON

STRANRAER. Perhaps no other town in South-west Scotland has done so much to make itself over for the tourist trade as Stranraer has. It used to be a rather notorious place, best known for its stinking Clayhole Bay. That is now long gone, and Clayhole Bay is a Holiday Centre, with most attractive gardens. Fortunately, so far at least, most of the old streets, narrow and winding, have escaped modernisation, and consequently the town is a pleasing mixture of the old and the new.

The old castle in the town, of which not much is left, dates from the early 16th century. Once, it was used as a prison for Covenanters captured by Claverhouse, and later as the town jail. Quite recently, a clutter of old and not very interesting houses has been cleared away, and replaced by gardens and flowers, so that the castle can be again seen in its proper perspective.

And of course Stranraer is the port for ferries to Northern Ireland. So it has all the excitement and bustle of major ports everywhere. Somehow one can never get enough of watching ships put out to sea — perhaps we are all Vikings at heart.

STRANRAER

WANLOCKHEAD The Museum of Scottish Lead Mining at Wanlockhead makes a very interesting day out from Dumfries or Castle Douglas.

Travel north by the A 76 Dumfries — Kilmarnock road, and turn right at Mennock on to the B 797 for Leadhills. The name 'Leadhills' really tells you what it is all about.

The A76 used to be the stagecoach road from Dumfries to Glasgow, and it passes through some lovely country. Long stretches of the De'il's Dyke can be seen to your left (if you are travelling north) by Sanquhar and Kirkconnel.

Drumlanrig Castle is near Thornhill, and in the village there is a pillar bearing a Pegasus — the armorial beast of the Duke of Buccleuch, who owns Drumlanrig. It was so erected that the Duke could look out of his castle windows and straight into the noble eye of that mythical horse. However, during one of the wars with France, some French prisoners were given the job of moving the monument to a more convenient place, and when they had finished their task, it was found that they had so positioned it that the Duke no longer looked straight into the eye of Pegasus, but straight at the other end of the beast. The Duke was displeased, but it is said that the whole countryside relished the joke.

You leave the A76 road at Mennock, and turn onto the B797 for Leadhills and the Museum of Scottish Lead Mining.

Before reaching the museum, though, you drive through the strange Pass of Mennock, a miniature Glencoe transplanted from the Highlands. Although to make that comparison is hardly fair, because the Pass of Mennock has a starkness and beauty all its own.

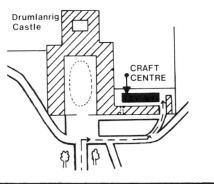

There is one quite long stretch of road where a tiny stream runs alongside, and you would willingly take an oath that the stream is running uphill. You will be convinced that you are going downhill, and yet the stream is going in the opposite direction. All very puzzling.

Wanlockhead claims (and the claim is disputed) to be the highest village in Scotland, and certainly it is finely placed, high in the Lowther Hills. For many hundreds of years lead has been mined here, probably first by the Romans. Where you find lead, you usually also find silver, and where you find silver, there is often gold, and where there is gold, sometimes there are precious stones. It all came together at Wanlockhead, and lead, silver, gold, diamonds, rubies and hyacinths were all mined thereabout. No wonder it was long known as *'God's Treasure-House in Scotland.'*

Today, though, after so many centuries, there is no more mining, and the ancient tradition is broken.

However, much remains of the old workings and plant, and they are very interesting. You can actually walk into an old drift mine and see the workings as they were abandoned more than a century ago, with the tool marks on the rocks. There is a great water-powered beam engine, beautifully restored, and the only one left in Britain. There are miners' cottages and tramways, and a great deal more.

It happened that rich Quaker families were the first to organise large scale mining there, and following the best Quaker traditions of humanity, they did not adopt the more rigorous (some would say inhumane) practices of the coal mine owners of Southern Scotland. The miners were not bound, serf-like, to the pits. Instead they were encouraged to read and study and 'better themselves'. There is still an impressive library used by the miners, who, with the slate miners of north Wales, were in their day the best-read workers in Britain.

A visit to Wanlockhead is most certainly a fine way to spend a day. And it lies in glorious country.

Drumlanrig Castle lies on one of the quiet side roads running off the A76 between Dumfries and the road to Wanlockhead. Drumlanrig is one of the great Stately Homes of Scotland, and, unusually, is open to the public. Few are in Scotland. Drumlanrig is the Dumfries-shire seat of the Duke of Buccleuch and Queensberry, and although itself not so old — late 17th century — it stands on the site of a much older Douglas stronghold. It is a startling, ornate structure, built in a pale pink sandstone, enormous and perhaps even overpowering.

As you can imagine, it was not exactly cheap to build Drumlanrig, even in the 17th century. It was the first Duke of Queensberry who built it, and it seems that he had not kept a close check on the costs. It is said that on his visit of inspection after the Castle was completed, he was so horrified at the cost that he spent only one night there, then hurried back to his comfortable old castle at Sanquhar, leaving the accounts scattered around the room, and crying: *'The De'il pike oot his e'en who looks herein!'*

The art collection alone would make a visit very worthwhile. There are, amongst others, a Rembrandt and a Holbein. The family portraits are endlessly fascinating — try to determine from them the character of the subject, and you will almost certainly be wrong.

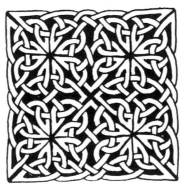

WHITHORN. Travelling down the peninsula from Wigtown, through pleasant pastoral scenery, one should certainly stop for a while at Garlieston, a quiet and typical seaside village on Wigtown Bay, before going on to Whithorn and the Isle of Whithorn.

The main attraction of Whithorn is without doubt the Priory. When you visit there, you are following in the footsteps of most of Scotland's famous (and infamous) figures. This was a place of pilgrimage almost from the day it was built in the early 12th. century. It was so popular, and held to be so holy, that it survived the Reformation, and a special Act of Parliament had to be passed to make pilgrimages there illegal.

It is the oldest Christian site in Scotland, and is believed to be on the same place as the even more ancient Candida Casa, the White House, of St. Ninian, and it was he who introduced Christianity to Scotland, and died at Candida Casa in 432 A.D. Seven hundred years later, in 1126, the Priory was founded, and much still stands.

Three miles south of Candida Casa, just by Isle of Whithorn, is St. Ninian's Oratory, a tiny, roofless chapel standing on a rocky promontory, buffetted by every wind that blows. It is a lovely spot, still a place of pilgrimage, and typical of the sites chosen by hermits and missionaries in those long-ago days.

Isle of Whithorn is a fine, albeit rather forlorn, village. It is not an island, in fact, but is the last village on the peninsula before land's end at Burrow Head. No packets call now at the Steam Packet Hotel. They once did, though, and this was a busy little harbour. Now, there is a little fishing, and not much else. That does not detract from its attractions for the holiday-maker, and especially so for the yachtsmen, for whom the little harbour is irresistible.

WHITHORN ABBEY

The writer Gavin Maxwell was reared in this area, at Monreith House, and it was one of his ancestors, Sir William, who founded the attractive village of Port William in 1770, and designed it as a holiday village, the first such in Scotland.

Monreith House, nearby, was built in 1799 as the Maxwell's family home, and in the grounds is a very fine Celtic cross, wheel-headed, and possibly 5th century.

Going north again, on the west side of the peninsula this time, there are the lovely Monreith sands, a great sweep of beach which holds all the attractions of beaches everywhere — beachcombing, lazing, swimming and sunning. And there is enough beach for everyone, and a lot left over. Here, too, is the unusual Gavin Maxwell Memorial, in the shape of an otter, reminding us of his deep affection for those long-persecuted animals.

ISLE OF WHITHORN

WIGTOWN. Although without the scenic grandeur of the Galloway Hills and the Mull of Galloway, the triangular peninsula of Wigtown is very much worth visiting for its quiet pastoral beauty, as well as for the many historical relics to be found there.

The Twentieth Century has almost passed by Wigtown itself, leaving it very quiet and dreamy, serving still as the market centre for the district, but no longer the busy county town it once was. To the visitor, the first and strongest impression is of the very wide main street, a street so wide that a bowling green and gardens run the length of it. It was not always thus. Once, the street served as a communal enclosure for all the domestic animals of the town, where they were shut up at night, in safety from marauders both animal and human.

Nearby is the touching Martyrs' Monument. Many Covenanters (and also, it should not be forgotten, many on the other side) were killed during the vicious struggle over church government in Scotland, when Protestants mauled Protestants as eagerly as ever Protestants mauled Catholics, or Catholics, Protestants. But none of the many martyrs for their beliefs seem to have caught the imagination, or touched the heart, so much as those two women who were tied to stakes and drowned by the rising tide of Wigtown Bay. Grierson of Lag, deputy to Claverhouse, ordered their execution in 1645. A sad story, and one still able to rouse emotions. Claverhouse, or Bloody Claverhouse, was also known to those on the other side of the struggle as Bonny Dundee. Today, take care not unthinkingly to whistle 'Bonny Dundee' anywhere in Galloway!

Only a short distance from Wigtown are the ruins of Baldoon Castle. David Dunbar lived there, he who married The Bride of Lammermoor, and thus inspired both Scott's novel, and the opera. The Bride herself came from Carscreugh Castle, just north-east of Glenluce. The marriage took place in Glen Luce church, and one month later Lucy died, mad, at Baldoon, in Wigtownshire.

Three miles away is the village of Kirkcowan, which somehow is almost the absolutely typical Galloway village, and most attractive. Near there is the enormous, evocative stone circle of Torhouse. There are nineteen great stones in the circle, which is 60 feet in diameter. It dates back some 4000 years, and is believed to have been a temple of the Druids.

LUATH PRESS GUIDES TO WESTERN SCOTLAND

THE LONELY LANDS. Tom Atkinson.

A guide book to Inveraray, Kintyre, Glen Coe, Loch Awe, Loch Lomond, Cowal, the Kyles of Bute, and all of central Argyll.
All the glories of Argyll are described in this book. From Dumbarton to Campbeltown there is a great wealth of beauty. It is a a quiet and lonely land, a land of history and legend, a land of unsurpassed glory.
Tom Atkinson describes it all, writing with deep insight of the land he loves. There could be no better guide to its beauties and history. Every visitor to this country of mountains and lochs and lonely beaches will find that enjoyment is enhanced by reading this book.
ISBN 0 946847 10 3. Paperback. Price: £2:00p.

ROADS TO THE ISLES. Tom Atkinson. A guide-book to Scotland's Far West, including Morar, Moidart, Morvern and Ardnamurchan.

This is the area lying to the west and north-west of Fort William. It is a land of still unspoiled loveliness, of mountain, loch and silver sands. It is a vast, quiet land of peace and grandeur. Legend, history and vivid description by an author who loves the area and knows it intimately make this book essential to all who visit this Highland wonderland.
ISBN 0 946487 01 4. Paperback. £1:80p.

THE EMPTY LANDS. Tom Atkinson.

A guidebook to the north-west of Scotland, from Fort William to Cape Wrath, and from Bettyhill to Lairg.
This is the fourth in the series Guides to Western Scotland, and it covers that vast empty quarter leading up to Cape Wrath. These are the Highlands of myth and legend, a land of unsurpassed beauty where sea and mountain mingle in majesty and grandeur. As in his other books, the author is not content to describe the scenery (which is really beyond description), or advise you where to go. He does all of that with his usual skill and enthusiasm, but he also places that superb landscape into its historical context, and tells how it and the people who live there have become what we see today. With love and compassion, and some anger, he has written a book which should be read by everyone who visits or lives in — or even dreams about — that empty land.

To be Published Easter 1986.

OTHER RECENT BOOKS FROM LUATH PRESS.

HIGHLAND BALLS AND VILLAGE HALLS.
G.W. Lockhart.

There is no doubt about Wallace Lockhart's love of Scottish country dancing, nor of his profound knowledge of it. Reminiscence, anecdotes, social comment and Scottish history, tartan and dress, prose and verse, the steps of the most important dances — these are all brought together to remind, amuse and instruct the reader in all facets of Scottish country dancing. Wallace Lockhart practices what he preaches. He grew up in a house where the carpet was constantly being lifted for dancing, and the strains of country dance music have thrilled him in castle and village hall. He is the leader of the well-known Quern Players, and he composed the dance *Eilidh MacIain*, which was the winning jig in the competition held by the Edinburgh Branch of the Royal Scottish Country Dance to commemorate its sixtieth anniversary.

This is a book for all who dance or who remember their dancing days. It is a book for all Scots.

ISBN 0 946487 12 X. Price: £3:75p.

WALKS IN THE CAIRNGORMS. Ernest Cross.

The Cairngorms are the highest uplands in Britain, and walking there introduces you to sub-arctic scenery found nowhere else. This book provides a selection of walks in a splendid and magnificent countryside — there are rare birds, animals and plants, geological curiosities, quiet woodland walks, unusual excursions in the mountains.

Ernest Cross has written an excellent guidebook to these things. Not only does he have an intimate knowledge of what he describes, but he loves it all deeply, and this shows.

ISBN 0 946487 09 X   Paperback.   £1:80p

THE SCOT AND HIS OATS. G.W. Lockhart.

A survey of the part played by oats and oatmeal in Scottish history, legend, romance and the Scottish character.

Sowing and mowing, stooking and stacking, milling and cooking, they are all in this book. Wallace Lockhart's research has carried him from Froissart to Macdiarmid, and his recipes range from an oatmeal *aperitif* to oatmeal candy. His stories about oats traverse the world from Mafeking to Toronto.

ISBN 0 946487 05 7.   Paperback.   Price £1:80p.

POEMS TO BE READ ALOUD: *A Victorian Drawing Room Entertainment.* Selected and with an Introduction by Tom Atkinson.

A very personal selection of poems specially designed for all those who believe that the world is full of people who long to hear you declaim such as these. The Entertainment ranges from an unusual and beautiful *Love Song* translated from the Sanskrit, to the drama of *The Shooting of Dan McGrew* and *The Green Eye of the Little Yellow God*, to the bathos of *Trees* and the outrageous bawdiness of *Eskimo Nell*. Altogether, a most unusual and amusing selection.

ISBN 0 946487 00 6. Paperback.   Price £1:80p.

THE BLEW BLANKET LIBRARY

The Blew (or Blue) Blanket was the privileged insignia of the craftsmen of Edinburgh in the time of James III. It was pledged to them by Privy Seal in 1482 when the craftsmen of the city, together with the merchants and other loyal subjects, marched on Edinburgh Castle and freed their King. It remained their insignia for centuries, and one of the original *Blew Blankets* is today in the Museum of Antiquities in Edinburgh.

The Blew Blanket Library is a collection of new books on Scotland by Scottish writers. Its aim is to provide a forum where writer-craftsmen of all types can display their wares in the context of Scotland today.

Already available in *The Blew Blanket Library*.

THE CROFTING YEARS. Francis Thompson.

A remarkable and moving study of crofting in the Highlands and Islands. It tells of the bloody conflicts a century ago when the crofters and their families faced all the forces of law and order and demanded a legal status and security of tenure, and of how gunboats cruised the Western Isles in Government's classic answer.

Life in the crofting townships is described with great insight and affection. Food, housing, healing and song are all dealt with. But the book is no nostalgic longing for the past. It looks to the future and argues that crofting must be carefully nurtured as a reservoir of potential strength for an uncertain future.

Francis Thompson lives and works in Stornoway. His life has been intimately bound up with the crofters, and he well knows of what he writes.

ISBN 0 946487 06 5. Paperback Price: £3:00p.

TALL TALES FROM AN ISLAND. Peter Macnab.

These tales come from the island of Mull, but they could just as well come from anywhere in the Highlands or Islands.

Witches, ghosts, warlocks and fairies abound, as do stories of the people, their quiet humour and their abiding wit. A book to dip into, laugh over and enthuse about. Out of this great range of stories a general picture appears of an island people, stubborn and strong in adversity, but warm and co-operative and totally wedded to their island way of life. It is a clear picture of a microcosmic society perfectly adapted to an environment that, in spite of its great beauty, can be harsh and unforgiving.

Peter Macnab was born and grew up on Mull, and he knows and loves every inch of it. Not for him the 'superiority' of the incomer who makes joke cardboard figures of the island people and their ways. He presents a rounded account of Mull and its people.

ISBN 0 946487. Paperback. Price: £3:95p.

THE EDGE OF THE WOOD. Alan Bold.

This is Alan Bold's first solo collection of short stories, and it is an impressive one. Here we have tales of the Scottish reality of today, tales told by a master craftsman. It is a fine collection, ranging from murder in a Scottish village to a Black Hole in Space, from a man's love for his dog to a young poet's first love and first poem. One of Scotland's foremost writers of today, Alan Bold has produced a collection of short stories which illustrate, through the eye of an artist, many of Scotland's current problems and contradictions.

ISBN 0 946487 08 1.   Paperback.   Price £4:25p

THE JOLLY BEGGARS OR LOVE AND LIBERTY.

Robert Burns. A facsimile of the original handwritten copy by Burns himself, with the poet's corrections.

This unusual volume contains not only the original text, but also the printed text on facing pages, and another text with glossary. It contains all the songs and music, and they are newly illustrated by John Hampson, a young Scottish artist of great promise. There is a long Introduction by Tom Atkinson, and an Essay on *Poetry, Politics and Forgetfulness* by William Neil, himself a poet of South-west Scotland. Although but little known today, *Love and Liberty* contains some of Robert Burns's most brilliant poetry and most lively songs. It was Scotland's poet at the height of his genius and power.

This Volume should certainly be on the shelves of every lover of Robert Burns.

ISBN 0 946487 02 2.   Casebound.   Price £8:00p.

WILD PLACES. William Neill.

Publication of these new poems and broadsheets by William Neill marks a very important step in contemporary Scottish letters. Writing in English, Scots and Gaelic, and translating between them, William Neill brings a strongly disciplined vision to bear on his native land. The lyricism and freedom of his language is matched by the beauty of his imagery, and to that imagery he brings the fruit of Scotland's three linguistic cultures. From such a synthesis has sprung poetry of a strength and virility rarely matched.

ISBN 0 946487 11 1.   Paperback.   £5:00p

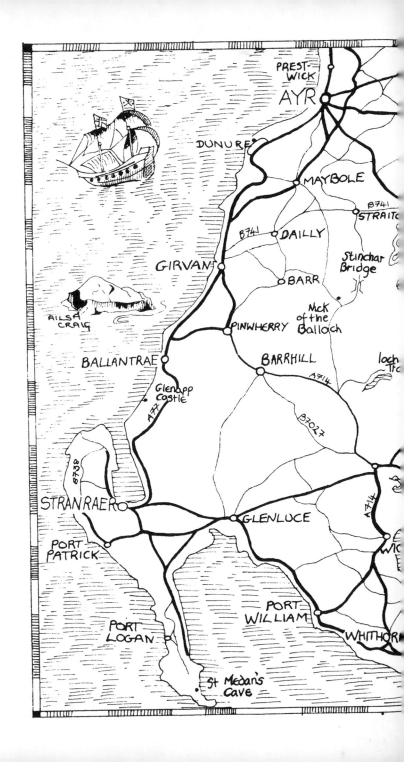

PREST-
WICK
AYR

DUNURE

MAYBOLE

B741
STRAITO

B741
DAILY

Stinchar
Bridge

GIRVAN

BARR

Nick
of the
Balloch

AILSA
CRAIG

PINWHERRY

BALLANTRAE

BARRHILL

A714

loch
Tro

Glenapp
Castle

A77

B7027

B739

STRANRAER

GLENLUCE

A714

WIC

PORT
PATRICK

PORT
WILLIAM

WHITHOR

PORT
LOGAN

St Medan's
Cave

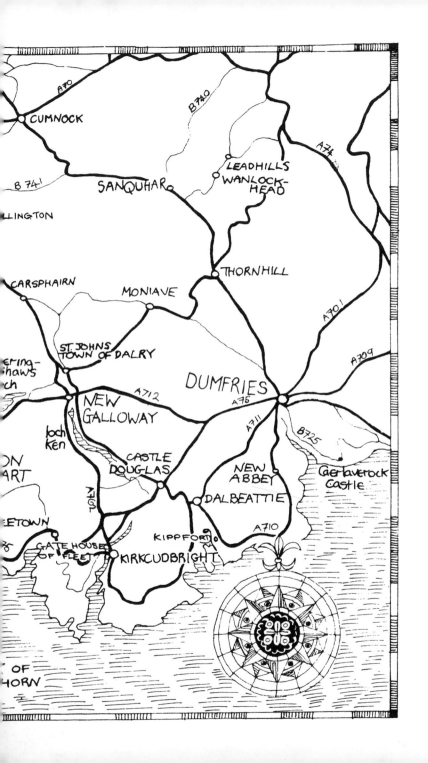